Praise for
Kim and Troy

"Troy and Kim Meeder are two of the m..... p... p
lege of knowing. A year ago my wife, Shirley, and I visited their nine-acre
Crystal Peaks Youth Ranch in Bend, Oregon, where they introduce dozens of wounded and needy children to abused and neglected horses. The
healing and mystical bond that occurs between the animals and soul-
hungry kids is wonderful to behold. Moreover, Kim and Troy do everything in the name of the Lord. I admire these people greatly and wish
somebody would give them a larger ranch on which to do their marvelous
work! I've seen nothing quite like it."

—JAMES DOBSON, PhD, *Family Talk*

Praise for
Fierce Beauty

"Kim Meeder poured her heart onto these pages, encouraging readers to
be authentic, to defend their hearts against sin, and to find peace in unexpected places. In *Fierce Beauty* you will be challenged to embrace God's
unconditional love when faced with roadblocks. Kim's words will inspire
you to stand up and run your own race—straight into the open arms of
Jesus. This book stands alone for self-study, and it would be an outstand-
ing choice for your small group."

—CAROL KENT, speaker and author of *Between a Rock and a Grace Place*

"Kim understands the fears and insecurities that plague so many of us—
even as women of God. With her unique combination of wisdom and
compassion, Kim encourages us to discover the life that God has called
us to, and to experience His peace in the process."

—DANAE DOBSON, author and speaker

"Kim Meeder knows firsthand the courageous heart adventure of healing. *Fierce Beauty* will empower you to recognize your surrender to the
King as the most powerful road to purpose, strength, and beauty."

—DR. JULI SLATTERY, author, family psychologist, *Focus on the Family*
    co-host

"*Fierce Beauty* is a breathtaking read from the first page to the last. With
a writing style that pierces the heart like exquisite poetry, Kim Meeder

tells a story filled with life-changing honesty and often startling "fierce beauty." Ultimately, it celebrates the resiliency of the human heart and God's power to change us, no matter the trials or heartaches of the past."

—Diane Noble, award-winning novelist

"Through tantalizing true-life tales, Kim Meeder captivates our interest and takes us to the edge of amazing experiences, then steers us to our heavenly Father for His love, mercy, and *hope!*"

—Suzanne Maurer, producer of the television documentary *Courage to Live: The Story of Charlie and Lucy Wedemeyer*

"Kim Meeder is an inspiration and tells her life stories with such compelling, faithful insight that even the hardest heart will be converted."

—Senator Chris Telfer

"In *Fierce Beauty,* Kim Meeder shares inspiring examples of what a difference our choices make. When we surrender and trust in the Lord, He gives us His hope. Choosing to stand for what matters most gives inner peace and strength to help us through each day's challenges. By doing so, our choices blaze a trail for others to follow."

—Diane Nelson Nye, wife, mother of seven, four-time survivor of breast cancer, currently battling stage IV cancer

"In *Fierce Beauty,* Kim Meeder recounts lessons learned through her own journey and awareness of God all around her. Her words will open your heart to receive and embrace truth from God's Word that is able to set even the most captive heart free. I was challenged and encouraged and am certain you will be too!"

—Meredith Andrews, recording artist

"Kim's gift for storytelling made me feel as if I were there, seeing it all with my own eyes. I highly recommend *Fierce Beauty* to all God's daughters, that they might see themselves as God sees them, and to His Sons, that they might see the women in their lives through God's eyes."

—Renee D. Godoy, senior pastor of Glad Tidings Church

"Kim inspires readers not only to see the beauty of the world but also to see the beauty in each God-created person and to see the real beauty in a soul set free through God's amazing grace. What an affirming message Kim offers in this treasure of a book!"

—Nancie Carmichael, author of *Selah* and *Surviving One Bad Year*

Choosing *to* Stand
for What Matters Most

FIERCE
BEAUTY

kim meeder

author of *Hope Rising*

MULTNOMAH
BOOKS

Fierce Beauty
Published by Multnomah Books
12265 Oracle Boulevard, Suite 200
Colorado Springs, Colorado 80921

ISBN 978-1-60142-203-3
ISBN 978-1-60142-204-0 (electronic)

Cover design by Laura Barlow

Published in association with the literary agency of Alive Communications Inc., 7680 Goddard Street, Suite 200, Colorado Springs, CO 80920, www.alivecommunications.com.

Published in the United States by WaterBrook Multnomah, an imprint of the Crown Publishing Group, a division of Random House Inc., New York.

Multnomah and its mountain colophon are registered trademarks of Random House Inc.

Library of Congress Cataloging-in-Publication Data
Meeder, Kim.
  Fierce beauty : choosing to stand for what matters most / Kim Meeder. — 1st ed.
    p. cm.
  ISBN 978-1-60142-203-3 — ISBN 978-1-60142-204-0 (electronic)
  1. Christian women—Religious life. I. Title.
  BV4527.M4374 2011
  248.8'43—dc22
                          2011013982

Printed in the United States of America
2013

10 9 8 7 6 5

Special Sales
Most WaterBrook Multnomah books are available at special quantity discounts when purchased in bulk by corporations, organizations, and special-interest groups. Custom imprinting or excerpting can also be done to fit special needs. For information, please e-mail SpecialMarkets@WaterBrookMultnomah.com or call 1-800-603-7051.

This book is dedicated to my precious assistant, sword bearer, mirror, encourager, and friend: Jenni Reiling.

In this life no one has taught me more about choosing joy than you. Throughout our friendship your consistent willingness to pick up the sword of joy has challenged me. I've watched you wield this beautiful weapon with the skill of a warrior.

Through sun and storm, your sword never lowered. Nor did your grip loosen when confronted with a horrifying array of adversaries, including pancreatic cancer. This fearsome opponent measures life not in years or months...but days.

You never asked, "Why me?" Instead your battle cry rang, "Why not me!" You ran to the fight and engaged death with the two-edged sword of encouragement and joy. Like the fearless men and women listed in the great hall of faith in Hebrews 11, you chose to stand fast and hold ground for our Lord.

Your eyes were fixed not on your cancer but on your King— so more would know of His saving grace.

Thin, weak, and bald, or even when regrowing soft, downy hair like that of a newborn lamb, you were still one of the most powerful, beautiful women I've ever known. While in the fight of your life, you remained focused solely on the hope of Christ.

You brandished the unfailing weapons of God, stood firm, and waged a ferocious battle for Him. My friend, because of your fierce, beautiful, and courageous example, you have inspired this book, and it has been titled in your honor.

Because of the hope of Jesus, I will love you forever.

Jenni Reiling
June 26, 1962–January 2, 2011

Contents

PART 3: THE WARRIOR

STANDING FOR WHAT MATTERS MOST

Friend, what is sacred to you? What would you fiercely defend?

I've asked myself these questions many times. Though I love God and the life He's given me, including all He's calling me to do, I haven't always felt this way.

There've been many seasons when my focus shifted away from God and toward myself. During these times my faith grew casual, which was dangerous for me. My life mirrored a defiant creature I once encountered.

While my sister and I were walking down a dirt road, we came upon a gopher snake. It was stretched out across the road, gathering all the warmth it could. Unfortunately, what felt good to the snake was not good. If it stayed to bask in this location, the next passing vehicle would crush it.

Not wishing for this beautiful creation to meet such an end, I decided to guide it out of harm's way. With my boot I carefully pushed a small mound of sand against the snake, gently encouraging it to move off the road. The reptile complied for a short distance before changing its mind. Without warning, the snake attacked, striking my boot repeatedly. Despite its objections I did what was best for the annoyed critter and directed it away from certain destruction.

Suddenly I recognized myself in this picture. I turned to my sister and asked, "I wonder how many times I've reacted the same way to God when He's tried to move me away from my will and toward His." Like the snake, I've often unwittingly chosen a path into danger.

Thankfully, friends don't let friends lie in the road…and neither does the King who loves us.

A genuine friend uses her boot, either gently or firmly, to move us out of harm's way. A genuine friend doesn't tell us only what we want to hear; she tells us what we need to know. A genuine friend might even give you this book.

Because we live in a world that constantly batters women with the lie that how we look is far more important than who we are, we often need some help to move away from this dangerous falsehood and back toward what's true.

My prayer is that this collection of real stories from my life will provide some of that help. The first section is a challenge to evaluate what you're honestly living for. The second section is an invitation to discover the God who offers you His eternal love, hope, and purpose. The third is an opportunity to see how you can answer God's call and begin living the life you were uniquely created for.

Living to serve oneself is not pretty.

Only when we truly understand who our King is does our self-importance fade away. Once freed from our pride, we can see how our purpose in this life is simple: to know Him. Our God is not passive in His care for us. He is a consuming fire. His love for each of us is both fierce and beautiful.

Friend, God *is* calling you to be beautiful, but not in the way the world demands. It was never His desire for you to focus on looking beautiful—He wants you to *become* beautiful. Contrary to this world's declaration, you are far more than the sum of your exterior; you're a vessel for the Living God. He's calling you to take action, to become beautiful by casting down your "princess crown" of entitlement, to pick up your King's sword of encouragement and fiercely defend those around you who are losing their battle for hope.

By doing so, you become—in the eyes of the King—a fierce beauty.

Just as I persisted in moving the snake toward a better path, our King gently persists in moving you toward His will. Now you must choose what is most sacred, what you will defend.

You can strive for your own way—or yield to His and choose to stand for what matters most.

1

THE FRACTURE

One True Anchor

How had it come to this?

I was in no man's land—literally a place where no human being should be. Step by foolish step, my pride had brought me to this bitter, frozen end. Though the terrain was intensely beautiful, all that waited for me here was my own death.

At more than 14,000 feet, I dangled motionless above an infinite void. I clung with a white-knuckled grip to the only device that could save me, my ice ax. Hanging from a near-vertical sheet of ice only yards below a mountain summit, I was surrounded by a silent world of white.

The expanse around me no longer concealed the fact that this could be the exquisite location where my life would end. Frayed thoughts twisted around the clutter of all my what-ifs. Finally the noisy and confused voices within my mind stilled. All that remained of my broken ability to reason circled in my head like a lost boomerang, proclaiming with each weak pass the same whispered message:

How did it come to this?

One of the highlights of my life occurred when I was five years old. Seared like a brand on my soul, the memory of that moment fills me with heat even now. Earlier on that long-ago day, with all the determination and strength that a little heart could muster, I'd gripped the back pockets of my dad's 501 jeans. Like a human mule, he'd patiently towed his youngest daughter up her first mountain. At 10,457 feet, requiring a round trip of less than five miles, Mount Lassen's small volcanic summit is not much of a challenge for those who frequent the high places. But for a young girl, reaching its peak was a triumph of love and wonder.

While my dad and I sat shielded by a rock wall, I snuggled close to him for warmth. The wind seemed to resent the vertical detour demanded by this small volcano and screamed all around us. My hair whipped around my face in a frenzied mass of black knots. With nothing above us but sky, I huddled in awe, captivated by the wonder that swept down and away like a living, undulating quilt of unthinkable beauty. Distinct from anything forged by the hands of men, this exquisite mantle continued beyond human sight in a decadent tapestry. Great forests appeared as deep folds of green and rushed down to embrace a myriad of sapphire lakes. Caught up in Creation's never-ending flow, green eventually gave way to amber as forests poured into vast plains of golden grass.

The rapid compression of air moving over the volcano's peak created cloud spindles. The white wisps appeared before our eyes, danced wildly across the summit, and disappeared just as swiftly. I was certain my dad and I were the only two people on earth who saw them. Like translucent sprites they tumbled and rolled in captivating shapes. Through exuberant eyes I watched them call me to join in their frolic. They seemed to play from the beginning of their brief lives right up to their last twisting moments. Spiraling down into threadlike strands of white, they waved one last good-bye before dissipating forever into a heavenly ocean of blue.

That moment with my dad on Lassen ignited in my heart a deep and passionate love for the mountains. There was an indescribable, fierce power in these high places—and also incredible wonder and beauty. I was hooked.

Later, more favor poured into my life when my dad was hired as a weekend downhill ski instructor on the lower flanks of northern California's Mount Shasta. At 14,162 feet, Shasta isn't the highest peak in the lower forty-eight states. But most agree that by sheer mass, it's one of the biggest. Shasta's base-to-summit rise of nearly ten thousand feet is second only to Mount Rainier and Mount Whitney in the contiguous United States. As an active, stand-alone volcano, Shasta dominates the horizon for more than one hundred miles in every direction.

Often I joined my dad in this impressive setting. I vividly recall one day hanging between his lanky legs as he held me under my arms. I stood on tiny wooden skis fastened with cable bindings to huge boots. "Ready, Kimbo?" my dad asked with the enthusiasm of a parent gifting his child with something he loves.

Together, we perched on the crest of what my youthful perspective saw as a daring precipice. With the pure, unshakable faith of a child, I looked at my dad's slender thighs and saw the trunks of two strong oaks. His grasp was firm enough to convince me that as long as I was locked in his protective embrace, we could ski through any peril. Had I glanced up, I'm sure I would've seen his superhero cape wafting majestically behind him. I braced myself by pressing mittened hands on the inside of each of his thighs. Like a pint-size copilot, I bobbed my head and said, "Okay, Daddy." We pushed off into a serpentine world of white, the beginning of many glorious weekends filled with father-daughter adventures.

That string of shared activities ended, however, much too soon. I was nine years old when the inconceivable happened. Divorce was tearing our family apart. My dad sought help in many professional directions, but, tragically, the help he so desperately needed was not to be found.

One day a friend of my father's picked up my sisters and me from school and took us to our grandparents' house. No one spoke. During that drive I knew something catastrophic had happened. At my grandparents' house a distraught woman tried to comfort me in her arms. She kept repeating, "I'm sorry. I'm sorry. I'm so deeply sorry." Finally she blurted out, "Your father has just murdered your mother and killed himself."

My first thought was that she was a liar. She *had* to be a liar because what she said simply could not be true.

I tore away and burst out the house's back door. I ran and ran through a small orchard until I fell, facedown, in the powdery, dry earth. I heard screaming and realized it was coming from me.

"Jesus, help me!" I cried. "Help me!"

And then, He did.

I didn't really know who Jesus was. I'd been to church only a few times in my life. Yet in that moment of despair, I somehow knew He was the only safe direction I could turn and if I didn't, I would die.

What I understand now is how on that terrible day the Lord of all Creation came and knelt in the dirt beside a breaking child. He reached down and took the small hand that reached up to Him...and He has *never* let go.

Only through His grace did I begin picking up the pieces of my shattered life. My sisters and I moved in with my grandparents and started attending church. In the years that followed, I learned that Jesus was my Redeemer and my shelter. Despite the grief and despair I faced, I always found comfort in Him.

Another of my refuges was the mountains. Once I began driving, I set about climbing every horizon—no matter where that horizon was. In these wind-chiseled cathedrals of stone, my heart felt truly free.

The subtle, mighty voice of breezes murmuring through ancient, high-altitude forests perpetually called me to come and rest within their boughs of peace. Heavy sorrows and burdens felt too weighty to follow me to these wild places. The farther I hiked, the farther behind I left my pain. I sensed that all the tragedies that gripped my heart were not strong enough to chase me into thin air. I scaled many of the peaks surrounding California's Redding basin. Once my husband, Troy, and I moved to Central Oregon, I climbed most of that skyline as well. The one glaring omission from my ascensions was Mount Shasta. Believing it would be too painful, I purposed in my heart never to go back.

It was on the pearly white shoulders of Shasta that my father reveled and refreshed and taught his youngest daughter to ski. Perhaps to seal his heart for the mountain he loved, my dad climbed this towering beauty the year before he died. Not long after, the mountain's original Ski Bowl lodge was destroyed. Adding to the Ski Bowl's woes was a constant siege of avalanches. More years than not, the upper chair towers were destroyed at random. In 1978 the destruction of the Green Butte chair towers was so devastating that the white flag was finally raised. Years later, a concrete lodge was erected on another side of the mountain.

There was no trace of the place where I fell in love with my dad. There was no reason for me to return.

Yet as time streamed by and my love for the mountains grew, an old calling circled within my heart. This familiar resonance beckoned me to the slopes of my youth. In a way that's difficult to describe, the baton of my dad's passion for the high places and this mountain in particular had passed to me. I realized it was my turn to stand on the frozen spire, the majestic summit of Shasta.

I chose to face my past. As I stepped through this threshold of sorrow, I knew the climb would be an emotional reunion with childhood memories of my dad. What I didn't foresee was how much those memories would confuse and distort my judgment.

After extensive research and dialogue with those experienced with the steeps of Mount Shasta, I finally felt prepared for the challenge. A friend and I began our ascent at 2 a.m. on the south flank. While demanding, this route was regarded as the safest and least technical way up, a good choice for a novice at this level of mountaineering.

Though it was June, on this climb my boots knew only the familiar crunch of melted and refrozen snow. We traveled by a single dot of light cast from my headlamp. Soon the lush darkness of the forest gave way to beckoning expanses of uninterrupted white. A waning, sickle moon offered little help, but the shimmering glory of a zillion stars demanded that I stow my puny light and walk under the illumination of their combined brilliance.

With the triumph of heaven reflecting off the mirror of snow beneath my feet, the world was transformed into a mighty, rising palace of silver splendor. Overhead, massive parapets of stone were draped in icy colors of royalty. Soaring in purple majesty, Sargents Ridge flanked my right, and the dark wall of Casaval Ridge rose to my left. Held between them, I was surrounded by their power. Beneath this starry robe every infinite detail of the mountain lay naked and unashamed for all eyes to behold its wonder.

Around 10,000 feet my friend and I climbed over a massive hump of snow mysteriously called Lake Helen. In my research I'd learned that only during excessive drought years does this phantom lake appear. Exhausted, my friend decided this reclusive landmark would be her summit.

The memory of my dad's voice, my enthusiasm, and my pride combined to drive me to the first major mistake of the day. I chose to climb alone on a big mountain I did not know. My friend and I mutually agreed to reunite in this exact place on my descent.

Setting out alone at a high altitude is never a good idea. I rationalized my dangerous decision by noting the handful of other climbers strewn about the pitch above me. My desire to reach the summit became all the validation I needed. I pressed on with crampons firmly strapped to my boots. My feet were armed with menacing rows of two-inch steel spikes. I'd need these weapons to defeat a new opponent: ice.

As I climbed, Sargents and Casaval ridges continued their rise as if to challenge each other in a collision of titans. Crushed between these towering foes was a steep snowfield, 2,500 feet in length and ominously named Avalanche Gulch. Walls of snow had already thundered down the ridges' flanks. Fresh avalanche tailings had cast alluvial fans of white destruction upon the same ravine I was trying to negotiate. The massive, rubbled remains were beautiful, intriguing, and frightening in equal measure. Weaving through their frozen skirts, the graveyard of ice gave silent witness to the awesome, foreboding power of the high places.

After an hour of crunching up the twisting and perilous incline, I stopped for a moment to relieve the tension in my calves and regain my breath. Instead, what I saw *caught* my breath. The sun was cresting the horizon on the opposite side of the mountain, sending the bulk of its hulking shadow nearly straight up into the heavens. Until that moment I'd never seen a shadow reach toward the sky. Lost in a view reserved for mountaineers, I stood transfixed as the shadow descended through the firmament to the slumbering earth below. The mountain's goliath silhouette, in perfect harmony with the rising sun, cast its swathed image over hundreds of square miles of Creation. Stretching like a visual prophecy, it joined the rising sun in heralding the imminent glory of this new day.

As the sun lifted in the sky, the mammoth shadow made a hasty retreat across the landscape below. It clung to the snowy slope for one last instant, then vanished completely as a laser beam of pure gold flooded down the steeps and consumed all darkness.

Washed in a baptism of new light, I felt the deep cold begin to loosen its grip. I continued to climb. Grateful for my ice ax, at 12,800 feet I safely passed through the vertical, crimson chimneys of compressed ash called the Red Banks. I knew this was the steepest part of the climb.

Immersed in irrevocable sunlight, I looked down the precipitous chasm to the east. I couldn't help but marvel at the gravity-defying tenacity of the Konwakiton glacier. So vertical was the rock to which it clung that the head of the glacier had peeled away from the cliff. Framed by melting teeth, the resulting moat of ice scowled up at me with a menacing grimace. Appreciative of the new and relatively mild grade, I continued up a section sardonically called Misery Ridge. My guess is that the exhausted soul who named this windswept spine believed that the crest above him was the summit. Though it looked like it, it wasn't (sad for weary legs). The true peak was still nearly a thousand feet above.

Finally I reached the summit rim. Like colossal pleats of a giant curtain heaving together, mighty ridges converged into a starlike pattern of immense, commanding beauty. The sheer physical power was overwhelming. Had someone been at my side, I doubt I would've been able to form words. This was as close to heaven as my feet had ever carried me.

Howling winds had carved strange and exquisite ice sculptures that adorned the frozen summit plateau. Among the nearly flat conjunction of arêtes, the true summit of this astounding mountain rose before me. Jutting fifty feet straight up into brilliant blue were the defiant remnants of an ancient lava tube. Fueled by exhilaration, I nearly ran across the lower summit col.

Though I knew of this extraordinary feature, I was still surprised to actually see it. To the left of the final buttress yawned an open, hissing cavern in the snow. From its boiling throat spewed a reeking, sulfuric stench. In a bizarre dichotomy, nature's opposing forces collided here. As unquenchable heat escaped the volcano's active core, the perpetual cold of this frigid altitude fought to extinguish it. The result was a sizzling cauldron of exposed basalt framed by a thick, glassy buildup of frozen steam. The continuous white plume rose in utter rebellion against the surrounding kingdom of ice. The combined effect was surreal.

Moving beyond what looked and smelled like an opening into the abyss, I glanced upward to evaluate the steep sides of the final buttress. Reaching high into a realm of cobalt, the jagged tower called to me. My ambition surged to a frenzied high. With a little more elevation, I would see "the box."

I knew from photographs that it was old and dented, fashioned of steel, and oxidized to a dull red patina. Held secure on the highest summit pinnacle, the box kept safe the book. The book kept safe the names— a record of those allowed to stand victorious in this honored place. It was the same place and the same type of book that, years earlier, my dad had signed.

The formidable frozen walls that soared above me were no match for the siren call of the book. Not seeing a clear route to the top, I looked for the other climbers, hoping to gain direction from them. None were visible. Driven by my fevered rush, I had passed them all earlier in the day.

At this point my lonely epiphany was clear: I didn't know which way to go.

Adding another link to my chain of foolish decisions, I chose *not* to wait for other climbers to guide me. I measured the wind-ravaged chimney with my eyes. It looked as if there was an uninterrupted section of steep but climbable snow that led to the summit.

I began my final ascent. With my ice ax firmly plunged into the frozen snow, I took two calculated strides, then checked the security of my crampons. Once assured, I removed my ax and plunged it into a higher position. I followed this purposeful progression until I had to relocate my ice ax with every increasingly perilous step. My anxiety climbed in mirrored unison.

I repeated this incremental method until I could step no more…until I could *move* no more! My novice aspirations had driven me into a no man's land. I was stuck. I was not on the pinnacle; I was hanging twenty feet below Shasta's icy summit on a glistening sheet of near-vertical ice. Now the only thing rising was my fear. I'd driven myself into a predicament beyond my ability to escape.

The slope was so steep that my left foot was placed nearly two feet above my right. I could clearly see that the slanted, two-inch ledge of ice that bore my left foot was fractured—it would *not* hold my full weight. I glanced over my right shoulder and saw nothing but blue. The ice was too steep to descend and too hard to ascend.

Standing with all my weight on my downhill foot, I fought my soaring sense of dread. Taking a few deep, steadying breaths, I evaluated my situation.

Blundering forward in selfish haste, I hadn't noticed that previous northwest winds had blown the steam up against the slope long enough to freeze the excess moisture into a sheet of nearly translucent boilerplate. If I tried to put weight on my uphill foot, the fractured ice beneath my boot would splinter away; I would lose purchase and fall. Because I was already thirty feet up the narrow chute and on a frozen surface with this high degree of angle, I understood that I wouldn't have enough time to self-arrest before I went into the sizzling cauldron of basalt. I would not fall on snow but rock. A clear picture materialized—if I fell, I would not survive.

For long moments I hung suspended over the void. With both hands gripping the shaft of my ice ax, I wondered—*How did it come to this?*

I realized that, in my haste and arrogant stupidity, I'd simply seen what I wanted and driven myself to obtain it. Nearly obsessed with the prize, I'd pushed reason aside. In the process I exchanged wisdom for foolishness—the first of many steps that often lead to death in the wilderness. Because my focus was only on what I wanted, I ignored the hazards.

I *knew* what I was doing was wrong. I simply chose to keep doing it anyway.

My pride and my foolish desire had brought me to this place—my pride in my climbing skills and ability to handle myself without help from anyone, and my desire to reconnect to childhood innocence, my father, his passion for this mountain, and his love for me.

I'd staked so much on obtaining these things. I'd allowed them to become my life's purpose, my value, my god. My sense of self-worth had become intricately woven into the design of this new selfish masterpiece.

It was clear I had chosen the wrong path. Hanging just below the summit, I had plenty of time to contemplate how I'd arrived at this perilous place. With a grip that made my knuckles ache, I held fast with both hands to the aluminum shaft of my ice ax. Slowly I realized this wind-tortured peak was *completely* still. There was not a breath of wind. The only sound was my own heartbeat thundering against my eardrums.

As minutes crept by, the cold air seemed to target my fists. I could not only hear my heartbeat from within, but I could also feel it pound inside each knuckle. Yet as uncomfortable as I was, I knew I had no option. I could not let go. If I let go, I would fall. If I fell, I would die.

I held on and waited.

Then, in the stillness, the familiar voice of my Lord quietly rose within my heart. *Child, if you would only hold on to Me like this. I am not a mere metal shaft; I am your King. I am your true Anchor. If you would choose to hold on to Me, you would know I am the One who always has— and always will—keep you from falling.*

I was ashamed. He was right. God designed me to cling only to *Him* with such lifesaving passion and determination. I needed to confess that it wasn't a metal stick that held me up. It was my Lord. Because I could move nothing else, I bowed my heart before Him and prayed. The prayer that streamed out of my heart was a simple confession of pride and a plea for help.

Jesus, help me… Please help me… Once again I'm reaching out to You. Although I've failed You miserably, You've never failed me. I'm sorry that I've chosen to serve the only other god there is—my desire, my will, my way. I've chosen to worship me instead of You. I'm so sorry for my awful pride and for how I've allowed it to block a close relationship with You. Will You forgive me, Lord? Will You wash my heart clean of my selfishness? Will You lead me again? I acknowledge that no matter how far I fall from Your presence, it's never beyond the depth of Your love for me. You've proven that You always have been and always will be with me. Again, Jesus, with this life, I choose to serve You.

In the moments that followed, something happened, something remarkable, something that changed my life. When I raised my eyes, I was still in *exactly* the same predicament as before. God didn't take my hardship away. God didn't fly me off to a safe place. He did something even better. He helped me realize that I was *in* a safe place—because He was with me.

He didn't take me out of my adversity; He took the adversity out of me. He revealed how He would go through the battle with me. I might fall; I might not. Either way, He was still my King, and I would trust Him with the outcome.

I knew what I had to do.

With my right hand I reached down and helped move my left foot down a few inches. From this new position I carefully sawed my crampons across the surface of the ice beneath my left foot. After several minutes of this, I had worn a groove that would hold half of the spikes on my boot. In one of the greatest acts of will I've ever known, I began to cautiously remove my ice ax.

Acutely aware of the vast expanse around me, I drew a deep breath and held it. Slowly I pulled my ax free from the only physical anchor I had. Exhaling steadily, I breathed another prayer of thanks to my Lord. The two-inch rim under my left boot held nearly all my weight.

Balancing almost completely on one foot, I moved nothing more than my eyes and left arm. By repositioning my ice ax slightly higher up the translucent incline, I would be in a stance to take another step. My unstable posture did not afford any leverage to drive my ax into a secure position. With my ax firmly clutched in my right hand and its strap around my wrist, I began tapping the spike into the ice with my closed left fist, using it against the ax like a hammer. This tedious process took nearly twenty minutes.

Finally, when my ax was securely driven deep into the ice, I slowly shifted my weight off my left foot to the new, higher position of my right. As all my weight shifted slightly upward, I repeated the entire process of sawing deep grooves into the ice with my crampons and repositioning my ax higher and higher. By doing so, I climbed the remaining distance to the summit. Though it was only about twenty vertical feet, it took nearly two hours to complete.

Emotionally exhausted, I crawled on trembling hands and knees to a safe nook on the summit spire. After shucking my pack, I leaned back against the frozen gray rocks and closed my eyes. It was only by God's redeeming grace that I'd survived the consequences of my foolish pride. I slumped, curled into a ball, and wept.

Once my fear and sorrow were sluiced by my tears, I slowly rose to my feet. While drying my face on the backs of my gloves, I noticed the box only a few feet away. Kneeling beside it, I reverently raised its heavy lid and carefully pulled out the book of names. I gently leafed through its tattered pages and found the last entry followed by nothing but white paper.

Out of His mercy, my heavenly Father had given me one last opportunity to repair the nearly severed bond between my earthly father and me. Though his life ended in horrific despair, he would forever be my daddy. I would always adore him and all he had imparted into my life.

Feeling again like a nine-year-old, I picked up a pencil and etched on the time-weathered sheet a long overdue letter of love to my dad. And beneath that entry, I wrote a message of deep gratitude to my God.

The Crossroad

We can fight for our way—or submit to His.

Friend, have you ever found yourself in a similar predicament—perhaps not literally clinging to a vertical sheet of ice, yet so committed to your personal path toward value and satisfaction that you suddenly realized you were on the precipice of death? Our need for self-worth and acceptance stalks each of us like an insatiable predator. And it can take so many forms…

Through desire or fatigue, some of us have bowed in submission to the distorted, self-serving *yuck* that constantly floods our souls through the media. By glamorous proclamations that we'll find personal satisfaction and romantic encounters and receive the attention and envy of others, we're lured into believing the messages we read in books and magazines. We're pressured to mirror the seductive imagery we see on television and movies. We're bombarded with catchy tunes and slogans calling us to conform to what we hear on the radio at our offices, schools, or homes. The message, though it varies in delivery, is simply this: if we will just succumb to this world's standard of beauty, we will have a purpose, we will have value, and we *will* be satisfied.

Meanwhile, some of us are seduced by the promise of comfort and pleasure from *things*. We accept the world's view that a higher-paying job, a bigger house, a trendy college, a newer car, and a flashier wardrobe will provide fulfillment. We buy into the narcissistic concept that wealth and possessions are the handholds in our ascent toward happiness.

Please don't misunderstand; there's nothing wrong with wealth by itself. I know many who've done incredibly generous things with their financial blessings. Wealth only becomes dangerous when we value and seek it more than God. Unfortunately, this world twists our logic into the belief that we're somehow *owed* adornments—that money, possessions, beauty, and comfort are our birthright and anything less is simply unfair. We've adopted the mentality of a spoiled princess, of self-appointed royalty wearing a crown of entitlement that brings glory to no one but ourselves.

I can say from experience that choosing a life based on serving oneself simply does not fulfill. It places us outside the life we were meant for, looking in at all that could be. It leaves us feeling empty and alone. Useless. Worthless. Hopeless.

Stuck.

It's at this crossroad, when the life we've chosen seems to turn against us, that we are tempted to blame God. Instead, we must *seek* Him.

Each of us will know times when we'll ask, *How did it come to this? How did I get to this place of complete paralysis, hanging over what could very well be my ultimate ruin?* The trail of choices by which we come to such a dark place is as unique as every person who reads this book. Yet the answer for each of us is always the same.

Jesus Christ is the right choice at every crossroad and the answer to every question.

We worship a Lord who is both fierce and beautiful—fierce in the way He hates injustice and sin and fights on our behalf; beautiful in who He is and the way He shows us grace, mercy, and love. As believers, we're called to reflect Him and become fierce and beautiful as well. We were created to serve an eternal purpose—not to follow our mortal desires while wearing a crown of our making, but to follow the One who wears a crown of thorns. We were not made to live on the outskirts of a kingdom but to worship in awe at the throne of our King. We were not designed to be princesses of entitlement but warriors of encouragement, fighting to bring love and hope to the world.

Our calling is to let go of our crown of gems (our puny personal ambitions, desires, and agendas) in order to pursue our true destiny: His crown of thorns (the will of our King). By doing so, we discover the value, joy, and fulfillment He always intended for those who call Him Lord.

Even now the King is beckoning. May He strengthen you in your endeavor to serve less of yourself...and more of Him.

THE PROBLEM

2

THE DREAM

An Elaborate Prison

Once again I adjusted my pillow. It was a vain attempt to find a comfortable position, something I'd already tried countless times that night. After a physically and emotionally demanding day on the ranch, sleep was slow to come. Yet it did finally come, accompanied by the most marvelous dream... Or was it a nightmare?

Through the lifting haze of early dawn, I glimpsed her. Intrigue drew me nearer. She was the most magnificent feathered creature I had ever seen. She was a bald eagle.

Her distinctive features were unmistakable...and unusual. I marveled at how her white head shone with the glittering brilliance of sunlight moving across snow. Though dusky in color, her body glimmered with the luminescence of stars on the darkest night. Moving closer, I saw that a thread of pure gold encircled every flawless quill. Her beak was formidable, strong, and impeccably outlined in...crimson.

Shimmering in the day's first glow, an elaborate object surrounded her. The circular base of the structure was fashioned in the likeness of an ornate crown. A blinding array of prismatic lights reflected off precious stones that covered its facade. Seemingly forged from molten sunbeams, golden bars rose from the base of the crown and converged in a point slightly above the eagle's head. A brilliant diamond glittered at the peak.

Together the eagle and her crown radiated an iridized flame that seemed to waft outward in mesmerizing waves of translucent color.

She was an all-consuming beauty—she was perfect.

Perfect.

Her grandeur drew me toward her. Spellbound, I took one hypnotic step after another. As more details emerged, I noticed something else. Truth rose like morning mist in my heart.

I'd been so captivated by her splendor that I hadn't fully realized she was indeed a *captive.*

The exquisite nature of her confinement veiled the fact that she was a prisoner. Her entrapment denied the eagle her birthright, her God-given liberty, and her purpose.

Adding to the eagle's woe, the golden cage was much too small. To fit within the glorious enclosure, her powerful back and shoulders were compromised downward. Her razor-sharp talons were painted in confusing patterns and were absurd in length, garish and glossy from lack of use. The screaming voice of freedom that must have once filled her chest and split the sky now was silenced by the luxurious hell imprisoning her.

Slowly she turned to look at me.

The piercing eyes that surely used to reflect fiery passion for life and the brilliance of her Creator now mirrored only a withering image. Her shallow vision had narrowed to a single harrowing convergence—*herself.*

The eagle's glory, her calling, her very life were ebbing with every weakened breath. I realized the crimson that stained her flawless beak had seeped from her corrupted heart. It was her own blood.

The eagle was dying.

My heart cried out for justice, for her release. *This should not be her end. She was free from the moment of her creation. She has a destiny, a future, a purpose to fulfill. She was designed for a calling only she can complete. She must fly!*

The eagle's eyes dimmed as her breath faltered. *"No!"* reverberated through my chest like an ancient war cry. I lunged toward the extravagant crown and attacked the perfection that was killing her. The brilliant confinement was cold—and *strong*. I strained against the jeweled bars, trying to spread a threshold by which she could escape. With jaws clenched I threw my head back, then screamed the name above all names: *"Jesus!"*

Instantly the combined light of a million stars flashed. Scorching heat surged over me. The bars began to yield, then exploded in a soul-shattering blast. Knocked backward, I watched in astonished wonder as a gaudy shower of splintered gold and scattering gems rained down through a cloud of shimmering dust.

The eagle? Straining to see through the ethereal haze, I saw her gasping—but free. She made no motion to rise. She appeared to be locked in place, somehow held in the same position she'd always known. She was free. She just didn't seem to believe it.

"Wake up! Wake up! *Wake up!*" I shouted while crawling toward her. The eagle blinked and stirred. After closing the distance between us, I gathered her in my arms and, with all my heart, soul, mind, and strength, threw the magnificent bird skyward. Instinctively she snapped open her illustrious wings. I watched the raptor catch the uprising current of pure encouragement that rose from my heart to hers.

"Fly! Fly! Fly, girl, fly!" I called out toward the heavens. With several strokes of her powerful wings, she soared upward. "Fly!" I continued to yell as I rose to my feet. She circled, perhaps looking for a greater updraft to fill her wingspan. Her wings rose and fell in mighty strokes, yet each appeared more labored than the last.

Confused, I realized the eagle was no longer rising. She was falling!

It was her adornments. The weight of her embellishments was more than she could bear.

The great raptor began to plummet. A weak cry left her chest, not of triumph...but of defeat. She was failing. After plunging in a nauseating spiral, she collided hard with the earth, landing in precisely the same place she had just escaped from, among the twisted remains of her former prison.

I watched in stunned silence. The eagle slowly roused, quietly disregarding me. Her only focus was concern over her radiant plumage. After careful inspection of every perfect feather, she appeared to be satisfied. Then the eagle glanced back and forth between earth and sky...*deciding*.

Appearing somewhat revived by her brief flight, a temporary luster rose in her eyes. The beautiful bird cast one longing gaze back toward the permanent glory of heaven and chose her fate.

With renewed resolution the eagle looked intently at the ground. Sifting through the glittering debris of what was once her lovely prison, she retrieved a fractured length of gold. Holding it close, she studied its brilliance. Speechless, I stood as a witness.

The eagle continued on her purposeful search. I watched, mouth agape, as the defeated raptor began to reconstruct—piece by alluring, glittering, captivating piece—the elaborate confinement that had once enslaved her.

The eagle was rebuilding her crown.

3

THE GIRL

Beautiful Like Jesus

"Look at me. I'm a princess!" the little girl said as she pointed to the ruffles that adorned her shirt. With surprisingly practiced rhythm, Carrie guided my attention to a sparkling necklace of faceted beads and matching bracelets that encircled each wrist. Without pause, ten perfectly polished pink fingernails were raised for my admiration. I smiled when I noticed her wrists were held high, with fingers draping downward in the universal "kiss my ring" position.

Over the next hour I watched this eight-year-old flit about our ranch like a confused butterfly not knowing where to land. She was scheduled to ride a horse, but that didn't interest Carrie at all. Sadly, nothing I had to offer satisfied her standards.

For years I've reveled in sharing with the kids who come to Crystal Peaks Youth Ranch, "If you go home clean, you probably didn't have any fun!" I'm quite certain this harkens back to my own childhood, when I was famous for skidding into the dinner table from parts unknown, completely out of breath. Often my grandpa looked across the table at me, shook his head, and exclaimed, "Good grief, kiddo! It looks like you've been running through the bushes to comb your hair!" Experiencing life was a good thing. I always counted myself extra lucky to bring home a few souvenirs. Whether they were stuck in my pockets or snagged in my hair really didn't matter.

In the sixteen years I've run Crystal Peaks Youth Ranch, I've come to realize that ranching and horses aren't for everyone, and that's okay. My little princess guest seemed to fall into this category. She ricocheted from one area to another, finding each venue as unsuitable to her liking as the one before. Soon her sweetness deteriorated into sour whininess.

"Euwwww, it's dirty!" she complained. "I don't want to ride, paint horses, swing, or play games on the grassy hill. My fingernails will get full of dirt!" As she spoke, she raised her palms so they faced her chest, and she spread her fingers. She circled aimlessly, looking like a sterilized, half-pint surgeon who couldn't find her patient.

Unfortunately, there was little that life on the ranch, or life in general, could offer her. Eventually Carrie settled on a small green bench nestled under a pine tree as the only place where she could remain clean and beautiful. Sitting quietly, she occasionally smoothed her shirt, examined the luster of her manicure, and carefully inspected every glittering bead that she wore. This seemed to be the best the young princess could do to fill her time. Meanwhile, her peers had an absolute ball daring one another to swim in the horse trough, striping their arms and faces with paint, riding ponies backward, and fully experiencing everything the ranch had to offer.

Although I checked often on the little girl, she rejected my repeated offers. She was determined to do whatever it took to stay beautiful. For the rest of the afternoon, she sat under the pine tree...completely alone.

Watching her, I couldn't help but think of another small "girl" who used to come to the ranch and sit alone. Her name was Amelia, and she often drove her two granddaughters to the ranch to ride.

Amelia was short and round with a cherubic, pie-shaped face. Her salt-and-pepper hair seemed to have a will all its own and framed her lively expressions in unruly waves. Her dark brown eyes gleamed with an impish twinkle that made me want to burst out laughing at a joke she'd yet to tell. Though her clothing was often old and too large for her small stature, she accessorized every outfit with something beautiful, something that always matched—a big bright smile. Amelia's playful attitude seemed to beckon the wounded to rise up and dance. Often I imagined her leading a joyful procession. I'm certain she would have…if she *could* have.

Amelia was crippled. A bout with polio during childhood had rendered her lower body nearly useless and caused her great pain. Even with the support of bulky leg braces, each step was accompanied by throbbing pangs. Simply getting in and out of the car, something most do without thought, was for Amelia an ordeal that took considerable planning. Yet mechanical assistance, walkers, canes, and lifelong pain were not enough to diminish the pure beauty of this amazing woman.

Upon her every arrival at the ranch, Amelia steered through the main gate and blessed me with a gigantic smile and kisses blown in my direction. Since she was so small, her welcome barely cleared the dashboard. Her chin was always held high, not in arrogance, but out of necessity to see over the steering wheel. She drove a worn-out white sedan that reminded me a little of her—it displayed some rust and a few dents yet somehow managed to faithfully get where it needed to go. Amelia always parked by the ranch trading post. It was a happy place that offered the best view of the hitching and riding areas and of the Cascade mountains in the distance.

"Kim, Kim!" she would hail in a heavy Spanish accent. Motioning with her hands, she would summon me to lean through the driver's open window and hug her. With most of my torso stuffed in the narrow space, we laughed like little girls and reveled in a moment of simply being together. Never did I miss the opportunity to tightly embrace this triumphant sprite.

The attribute I loved most about Amelia was her brilliant attitude: she never surrendered to her quiet life of pain. In her mind the social health and well-being of her shy grandbabies far outweighed her own ease or comfort. With what appeared to be unlimited patience, she sat in her car and watched them enjoy our horses for hours.

One summer afternoon I stood waiting for my precious little friend to make her way up the ranch driveway. It was hot, and the light afternoon breeze was a gift to the back of my neck. Hearing the sound of tires crunching through gravel, I turned to look down the hill and saw Amelia's car approaching. As soon as I saw her face, I knew something was wrong. The trademark smile was missing, along with the usual kisses blown my way. Even my window greeting did little to lift her somber mood. After some honest questioning, the source of her sorrow finally ebbed out in a trickle of painful words.

"There is nothing that I can do, nothing that helps this wonderful place," Amelia said. "Everyone who comes here helps by doing something, yet here I sit, able to do nothing."

My heart withered under the weight of Amelia's distress. As if polio hadn't already taken enough from her, now it threatened to rob her joy as well. The discouragement she expressed lay in gloomy contrast to her usually sunny spirit. Even after my strong rebuttals, she left the ranch a few hours later, looking as defeated as when she had arrived.

Two weeks passed before Amelia returned. This time I was relieved to see that she was her bright, waving-and-blowing-kisses self again. She pulled her car to a stop in her favorite place and could not roll down her window fast enough. Moving her mouth up to the opening window, she triumphantly declared, "I finally found what I can do!"

Before I could reply, she turned away from me. By the time I reached her car door, she'd turned back around and now held an enormous plate of homemade sugar cookies. She lifted the platter until it nearly collided with her chin. Amelia beamed with such brilliance that her delight poured over me like a warm, living wave. All she wanted to do was help, and by finding a way, her joy was released for all to benefit.

With a broad smile, Amelia presented me with another offering—words that carried more wisdom than I may ever possess. She looked up into my face and said, "If everyone does something, even a little thing, only then will the mountains move." Just like that my friend imparted to me a life-changing truth—a pearl of wisdom about the size of Jupiter!

With a bob of her chin, Amelia directed me to take one of her cookies. After retrieving the treat, I glanced around the ranch. It was alive with children, many who hadn't had a cookie—or any gift—in a long time. Undeterred by her limitations, Amelia intended to bless each one with a sweet little present made only for them. When I heralded the arrival of the cookies, several kids seemed perplexed. One little boy asked, "Why would someone who doesn't even know me want to give me a gift?" I answered loud enough so Amelia could hear me: "Because she wants you to know that you are very special and that she cares about you."

The little boy cautiously walked over to her car door and watched other kids receive a sugary snack. Amelia noticed him and asked, "Young man, would you like a cookie too?"

He nodded soberly. Amelia encouraged him further by saying, "How about this one?" as she pointed to a cookie that seemed to have a bit more frosting than the others. His face lit up with more than a little disbelief. "Really? You made this *just for me*? Wow!" After accepting her gift, the boy stared alternately at the treat and Amelia. His innocent expression indicated he believed he'd just witnessed his first miracle.

Few people would look at Amelia and anticipate a miracle. If they judged her by her appearance, they wouldn't expect much at all. By the world's standards of beauty, Amelia simply wouldn't measure up. Her focus, however, was not on how she looked but how she lived.

Yet the little boy and I both saw Amelia as *radiant*. Her selfless actions proclaimed an entirely different kind of beauty. Out of so little, she gave so much. Though her life was daily shrouded in pain, she chose to live beyond its exhausting reach.

Amelia chose to fight through her difficulties and become a blessing to others...to be beautiful from the inside out.

True Beauty

We often chase after this world's definition
of beauty and value and reject genuine worth
offered by our Lord. Will we live in fantasies
of our own creations or choose God's best
purpose for our lives?

Like the little princess who chose to sit alone, many girls who come to our ranch love to play make-believe. It can be a harmless and healthy way of growing the imagination. Many adults do the same thing. Sadly, unlike the little girls who know they're playing make-believe, the grownups often do not. Women are not simply creating fantasies to stretch their imaginations; they're *believing* them.

Ladies, when did we become so shallow? How long have we embraced the great lie, the sad declaration that how we look is more important than who we are? On what grim day in history did we surrender to our selfishness and begin bowing before our own reflections, becoming little more than slaves to our desires?

Why do we choose to exchange the ability to love and care for others for the crushing low of merely loving and caring for ourselves? Throughout the ages women have been *lied* to. Unfortunately, we're still choosing to believe the lies!

Daily, this world challenges our equilibrium to the point of wreckage. We're pressured by the media in all its forms to accept misguided standards of what is lovely, moral, and satisfying. For many of us, these lies have been so deeply rooted in our every fiber that the hollow pursuit of physical beauty has become our god. As a result, scores of women now view life through eyes so dim that all they see is a horizon filled with their own darkened perspective of beauty. Many have become so dull that all they feel is a painful sense of lack.

The truth is, we have it all backward!

God's definition of beauty is not from the outside in…but the inside out. His Word says, "You should be known for the beauty that comes from *within,* the unfading beauty of a gentle and quiet spirit, which is so precious to God" (1 Peter 3:4). Because of this truth, all our efforts to beautify our external facade can *never* fix or cure an inside ugliness. If our inside is broken, no amount of exterior renovation will restore it.

The day we called Jesus Christ "our Lord," we accepted His invitation to become a fledgling warrior of truth for Him. For too many of us, however, the young warrior within is not growing into a mighty force for our King. For thousands of Christian women, it isn't growing at all. Instead, the warrior we were meant to be is joining a nation of self-entitled princesses: "They will betray their friends, be reckless, be puffed up with pride, and love pleasure rather than God. They will act as if they are religious, but they will reject the power that could make them godly…. Such women are forever following new teachings, but they never understand the truth…. Their minds are depraved, and their faith is counterfeit" (2 Timothy 3:4–5, 7–8).

God *is* calling women to be beautiful, just not in the way our world portrays. God's desire is that we will choose to lay down our princess crown of entitlement, pick up His sword of encouragement, and start fighting for those around us who are losing their battle for hope.

God help us. The fact is that from the beginning of history, *He has never stopped trying.*

Friend, sin is not pretty.

However, righteous beauty is like a sunrise; it cannot be stopped no matter what circumstances surround it. It is not affected by the weather of perceived emotions. It is stable, secure, and dependable. It does not merely sparkle from the outside in; it radiates from the inside out, because it's inside these perishable containers that the glory of our Lord is held. This glory—*His glory within us*—is what makes us beautiful.

Like Carrie, the frilly little guest at our ranch, Amelia was another "little girl" who came to the ranch searching for fulfillment. Because she chose to experience life by serving others, she found a much deeper purpose. Amelia taught me so much the day she brought cookies. Even though it was difficult for her, she did it anyway. She pushed beyond her own desires and took action to lift the hearts of others. She demonstrated that true beauty is not about how we look. Authentic beauty is revealed in what we do for those in need around us. On that day I wanted to be beautiful like Amelia...because she was beautiful like Jesus.

Do you wish to be beautiful, as truly beautiful as Amelia? It's not so difficult. Authentic beauty is not based on what we're wearing or how we look. It flows out of our hearts and is a form of worship of our King. This beauty grows when we open our eyes to the hurting souls around us— our neighbors, our co-workers, our friends, our husbands, our children— and ask, "What can I do today to show them the love of Jesus?" The simplest act, even a kind word, is the first step toward a radiant beauty that will endear us in the eyes of the One who matters most.

4

THE ZIPPER

A Collision Course with Ruin

I'm a runner, but not in the way you might think. My staff would enthusiastically confess for me that the sole reason I run is to maintain my superhuman ability to eat busloads of M&M'S and still fit in my pants. I tell my running mates that I'm just preparing for the future. I happen to have insider knowledge about a technique scientists are closing in on—a way to bale M&M'S like hay and sell them by the ton!

For me, running is about fellowship and whom I'm jogging with. For the past two decades, I've valued this time so much that I've run a marathon roughly every other year. It's been a wonderful opportunity to spend precious time moving stride for stride with family and friends. Running 26.2 miles sounds lofty, but, trust me, it's not. If I can do it, anyone can. It's simply one of the things I do to stay physically and relationally fit and keep my life balanced. Especially since *balanced* has not always been true of me.

For propriety's sake, please understand that I use the word *run* as a figure of speech. At five feet nine inches and weighing an industrial 163 pounds, I believe the lithe grace one usually associates with *run* does not apply to the lead-footed lurching of my tyrannosaurish gait. Whether I'm running uphill, downhill, sideways, or backward, I'm the ten-minute-mile queen. Over the years I've been nicknamed "Diesel," in part because once I get warmed up, I'm completely comfortable chugging along all day at this humble pace.

Our marathon training schedule is simple. We run two short distances during the week and save the long jog for Saturday mornings. We add an extra mile each weekend until we reach twenty-four miles, and then, about a month before the race, we taper down sharply to the day of our big event.

Because of the heavy ranch schedule, the only marathons we can participate in are those held in the early spring. Nearly all our training is done during the coldest months of winter, my favorite season to run.

On one particular Saturday a few years ago, my running team and I gathered in the nearby town of Sunriver. We planned to run to Bend via a network of logging roads that eventually connect to a beautiful river trail. The course we mapped out was about twenty-two miles and was a point-to-point run. These are my favorite types of runs because they each offer a distinctive adventure. Once in the wilderness, our runners were to travel in pairs for safety. I advised all my teammates to be prepared for a variety of weather conditions and carry their own survival gear. At nearly 4,000 feet in elevation, the weather can change rapidly in the high desert. When beginning a long route, it's best to wear layers and then add or shed as the climate dictates.

Our run started under low clouds and heavy sleet. After we climbed a few miles and gained elevation, the sleet transformed into downy snow. The falling world of white swirled around me in soft eddies and churns. Each rolling flurry made me grateful for the new Windbreaker and gloves I'd just purchased. So far, the maiden voyage of this light jacket was proving it to be a useful acquisition.

True to the Central Oregon climate, it wasn't long before the sun's triumphant beams began to break though the falling snowflakes. I was awestruck by the rare phenomenon of being able to run hand in hand with my own shadow amid heavy snow. While ethereal beauty wafted down, my heart filled with silent praise: *Thank You, Lord, for this amazing world.* I smiled and wondered if this might be what the fringe of His robe would look like.

After several more uphill miles, I was warm enough to remove my

Windbreaker. I tied it around my waist and left the tail to drape over my backside. As one who loves to run in the cold, I've learned this is the best way to keep my "engine room" warm and moving well. While running, I was only vaguely aware that the zipper head of my jacket was gently drumming against the outside of my right thigh. Step after step, mile after mile, hour after hour, the nearly imperceptible tapping continued. It was no big deal. It was a zipper head, it wasn't even an inch long, and it weighed nothing at all.

Later that night I finally had the opportunity to jump into the shower. That's when I noticed it. As I raised my right leg to step into the tub, I was stunned by what I saw. My entire right thigh looked as if it had been beaten with a gunnysack full of golf balls. On my leg were approximately sixty dime-size bruises. I looked down at my completely purple thigh in astonishment. I've run for years with jackets tied around my waist and never experienced anything like this.

Yet the damage was done.

Clearly, the whipping zipper head was the culprit. Hot steam filled the room as I stood motionless on one leg. I found it hard to believe that such a weightless, insignificant little thing, left unchecked, could cause so much damage. Nevertheless, before me in vibrant color, was my proof that, indeed, it could.

Finally I stepped into the streaming warmth of the shower. It became a refuge for reflection, a time to consider how destructive "little things" can become. It didn't take me long to reel through a list of events in my life that began with an insignificant start and—swinging to the opposite extreme like a pendulum—ended with a damaging finish.

I was only thirteen when the serpents of image and appearance slithered into my heart. I was about to be a freshman at a new high school and would know few others. Feeling insecure about the unknown, I took stock of myself. One destructive example was set in motion by a single, simple thought: *Kim, you weigh too much. You would be healthier, faster, stronger, and much better to look at if you weighed less.*

Well, okay. I guess I should lose a few pounds.

A harmless observation, fueled by the stress of a destroyed family, soon grew into something far from harmless. Even though my grandmother's love for my sisters and me was undeniable, the trauma of my parents' deaths was a private tragedy for everyone; none of us was equipped for the sudden loss. Year after year I watched my sisters and grandparents struggle to deal with their grief in their unique ways. During that time our home often ricocheted between silence, volatility, self-imposed isolation, and brittle vignettes of peace.

We were on a crash course of learning how to walk through a season of unthinkable anguish. Our life as a family—something that should have felt safe and under control—repeatedly felt anxious and completely out of control. Many a night I lay in my little bed and listened to my grandmother through the wall that separated our bedrooms. She never knew that I could hear her crying herself to sleep. Her helpless sobs in the night became the only motivation I needed to never trouble her again. I purposed in my heart that my actions would no longer bring her grief. I would become the perfect child. I would be in control of my every word and action and never again cause her a moment of pain or worry.

It wasn't long before my warped need to control myself became my sole ambition, my sense of value, my lonely god.

What began as a healthy endeavor soon grew into an obsession. I lost five pounds, then ten, then fifteen, and suddenly earned the praise of all. At my school, job, and church, I gained more and more attention for my appearance. More than once I was stopped by virtual strangers who looked at me with tear-filled eyes and stammered, "Oh my goodness, you've become as slender and beautiful as your mother!"

Wow, who knew I was so good at this? I thought. *If some weight loss is good, more will certainly be better.* As a former chunky tomboy, this "reduction" suddenly gave me a sense of purpose. During a season that often seemed out of control, my weight became an area in which I felt powerful and in control. I liked that feeling; I liked it too much.

As my weight plummeted, my height skyrocketed. I grew six inches during my first two years of high school, topping out at sixty-nine inches.

My bones grew more heavy and dense as well. In my obsessed frame of mind, this caused a paradoxical problem for me. I simply could not lose control. I could not allow my weight to rule me, to win. Even though my height was that of the average American man and I had the bone structure to match, my weight often hovered around 113 pounds.

I became addicted to seeing the incremental lines on a scale, any scale, go down. I weighed myself up to twenty times a day. Often I did not drink water because this would cause an unacceptable increase in weight. I kept and chewed the same piece of gum for days, sometimes weeks, to save on my caloric total. More days than not, my lunch was a lone green apple.

My grandmother was an extraordinary cook, and when no one was home, I would chew up obscene amounts of food, spit the results into the sink, and wash the evidence down the drain. Cake frosting was my archenemy. It became a family joke. Only my sisters knew how many of my grandma's cakes I destroyed by quickly eating only the frosting.

Unfortunately, that's where the joke ended. If I momentarily lost control and swallowed too many bites of food, the immediate punishment I inflicted on myself was severe. Each transgression was punished with thousands of sit-ups, push-ups, and jump-rope skips. Even in this narcissistic exercise, I gained a weird pride in counting every single repetition. If I failed to complete the number in my head, I was sure I'd failed as a person and suffered an additional crushing mental defeat.

For five years I chose to live in this prison, bowing before my self-appointed deity. Though I was a believer and in a young-adult home group, taught a Bible study, and attended a Christian college, reigning supreme over all was my desire to be thin. It shadowed my every thought, determined every decision, and governed all my actions. I'd given my life over to my obsession with food.

Even though my words proclaimed otherwise, during this tormented season I did not trust in God. I trusted in me. My faith rested in my own sense of leadership. Under my rule I led myself to the brink of starvation. I was too weak to explore my beloved mountains or, for that matter, to participate in any sport or physical activity outside my near-daily punishments. My self-imposed weight loss devastated my once-healthy immune system. I was sick all the time. My vitality deteriorated so quickly that my long black hair started to fall out in clumps. None of this self-inflicted ruin deterred me from my goal—the goal of control.

To maintain my facade, I became a master at hiding my addiction. Not even my family knew. I came up with myriad excuses as to why I didn't have time to play anymore. I camouflaged my thinning hair with layered styles that looked bouncy and full. I never changed my clothes in front of anyone, not an easy task when being raised with two older sisters and having four years of PE classes.

If I knew I would have a sit-down dinner, I skipped all other meals that day. Often I hid the volume of what I ate by carrying my food into another room and secretly throwing it away. Once while scraping an entire meal into the garbage, my grandmother surprised me.

"Honey, what are you doing?" she said in a voice that demanded more than asked.

"Oh, one of my classmates brought some pizzas to our college class. Can you believe that?" I said. "It was such a fun surprise. I didn't want them to feel bad, so I ate some. I guess I'm just not as hungry as I thought I was. I'm sorry."

She frowned at me, her polite way of saying she didn't appreciate my not enjoying her meal and wasting it by tossing it in the trash. She caught me doing this at other times too. But I always had a quick answer. Even though I knew my grandparents were stretched financially, this knowledge was not enough for me to cease my utterly selfish destruction of the meals they offered me. My shell game with food became a daily routine, a clandestine challenge that I actually enjoyed. The simple fact that I could hide my indulgence in plain sight only fed my sense of power.

No one was going to stop me…and I didn't want to stop myself. Like the zipper head tapping against my thigh, what started as a "little sin" quietly tapped its way into destroying my heart, my life, and my relationship with my Lord.

Thankfully, there is no depth of sin we can ever know that is beyond Jesus' ability to reach when we genuinely cry out to Him.

It's not enough for us to recognize our plight. An authentically repentant soul is a person who chooses to actively move away from damaging habits and *toward* the Lord. We're not Christians simply because we call ourselves such. For me, being a Christian means turning away from my selfish, self-centered life and turning toward Christ and trusting Him to lead me.

It wasn't until I chose to put Jesus' plan for me above my own ideas that the shackles of my destruction were finally broken. This happened when the rules of my game were irreversibly challenged. When I was nineteen, I married the man of my dreams. Suddenly I could no longer hide in public or carry out my fanatical exercise regimes. I was now forever linked to a handsome, six-foot-three-inch mirror, who reflected how truly selfish and destructive my behavior had become.

I remember Troy saying during a heated conversation, "What you're doing is fake. It's a cheesy, man-made attempt at creating value. It's simply an excuse to become something you're not, something God never intended you to be. Your hands, feet, and bones are as big as mine. Of course you're supposed to weigh more than a kid. What you're doing isn't pretty; it's just selfish!"

Yet no amount of talking or counsel was going to fix what was broken inside my head. I was certain I was right, and no one on earth was going to convince me that I needed to change.

And no one on earth did.

It was the One from heaven who ultimately healed my brokenness. It wasn't until I chose to look intently at what I'd become that I finally realized my need for a savior. Most of my life I'd known the right answer, but I'd never fully embraced the *real* answer. It was no longer enough to know about Jesus. I wanted to *know* Jesus.

Though I could deflect human counsel by an internal rolling of the eyes, I could not hide from the raw, timeless truth of God's Word. As I started to read my Bible every day, its power began to systematically dismantle the lies I'd built into my heart, and my destructive habits were revealed. I wasn't righteous at all; I was selfish...incredibly selfish. By holding on to my obsession to be thin, I was telling everyone—including God—that I loved my appearance more than I loved Him. Once this fact flooded into my heart, I couldn't deny it, and I was deeply ashamed.

The change in my life was not instant. I grew by degrees, like a baby learning how to walk. I rose and fell countless times. But because I was honestly allowing Jesus' freedom and power into my life, I learned that I could always rely on Him to give me the strength to stand up and try again.

I had chosen to live in a prison of my own construction. Tap by tap, choice by choice, I nearly allowed my "little sins" to steal my life. It was only the truth of God's Word that released me, restored me, and gave me the answers I so desperately sought. Now I am thankful every day for the freedom I have in Jesus: "And you will know the truth, and the truth will set you free.... So if the Son sets you free, you will indeed be free" (John 8:32, 36).

LITTLE SINS

> Little sins allowed in our lives, over time,
> will cause great damage.

All of us have a nemesis that, left unchecked, will destroy us. Our problem is...sin.

We might think, *It's such a ridiculously small thing. I can stop any time I want to. It doesn't hurt anybody. It makes me feel good about myself.* When it comes to opening our lives to sin, our lists of excuses are long. As my battle with anorexia taught me, how we justify allowing these little "pets" into our lives is irrelevant, especially when compared to what they will do in our hearts once we say yes to them.

As a child, I heard a rhyme that impacted me so greatly I remember it to this day. It went something like this:

I heard a knock on the door of my heart's lonely inn.
"Who is there?" I called out.
"Oh, just a little lonely sin."
I opened the door and—all HELL came in! (source unknown)

Whether we acknowledge it or not, all sin destroys. As Scripture reminds us, it is like "a little yeast [that] spreads quickly through the whole batch of dough!" (Galatians 5:9). If something as minuscule and harmless as yeast can permeate and change an entire lump of dough, clearly our sin can do much more. Without a doubt, the garbage we allow into our lives is going to hurt us. Our sin will eventually destroy our lives. It will also devastate those whom we are called to care for. Even worse, it offends our King, because all sin is a form of rebellion against Him.

The truth is, no heart can rebel against God and draw near to Him at the same time.

Every believer has experienced times of feeling far from God. Often we inadvertently blame Him for the distance we sense when we're the ones who've continued to allow sin into our lives. This resulting distance isn't because He's left us; it's because we've left Him.

The Lord has said, "These people say they are mine. They honor me with their lips, but their hearts are far away" (Isaiah 29:13). No matter how good we think we are, we can never please God with our outward actions if our inward attitude is not right before Him.

If we confess our sin to God, like any good parent He allows us to bear the consequences of our waywardness while also adding His deep, abiding joy. God wants a close relationship with each of us. He's done mighty things to facilitate that. But, friend, we have to want that closeness as well.

All healing and redemption begin the same way. They start with a decision, a choice to trust Jesus more than our own understanding.

All those years ago I knew that if I was ever going to stop my self-destructive weight plan, I needed to fully embrace a leader with power greater than my own. My alleged power was a ridiculous joke compared to the eternal authority of God: "For the word of God is full of living power. It is sharper than the sharpest knife, cutting deep into our innermost thoughts and desires. It exposes us for what we really are. Nothing in all creation can hide from him. Everything is naked and exposed before his eyes. This is the God to whom we must explain all that we have done.... Let us cling to him and never stop trusting him" (Hebrews 4:12–14).

When we allow our faith to rest in ourselves more than in the Lord, we set in motion a collision course with ruin. When I was god of my own life, I nearly destroyed myself. My desire for personal control and acceptance by others became my paltry reward. For that little glittery tiara, I gave up my King's genuine freedom, love, peace, strength, and joy. It took honest advice from someone I loved and trusted—my husband—to help me begin to see how far I'd separated myself from my Lord.

As long as we're breathing, God's mercy and forgiveness have no expiration date. He never gives up...on any of us.

In my hollow tunnels of shame and guilt, the truth of God's Word brought the only genuine hope I knew: "And I am convinced that nothing can ever separate us from his love. Death can't, and life can't. The angels can't, and the demons can't. Our fears for today, our worries about tomorrow, and even the powers of hell can't keep God's love away. Whether we are high above the sky or in the deepest ocean, nothing in all creation will ever be able to separate us from the love of God that is revealed in Christ Jesus our Lord" (Romans 8:38–39).

Friend, we do have a problem when we choose to allow little sins to infiltrate our lives and tap away at our ability to mirror the glory and love of our King. If they are left unchecked, it's only a matter of time before our mirrors break.

Just as every little sin starts with a choice, so does receiving the hope, forgiveness, and life of our King. There is no place we can go, no damage we can do, no mess we can make that can prevent His redeeming love from finding, healing, and restoring us.

5

THE TURTLE

Plunging into Darkness

With my eyes shut beneath the faded brim of my ranch hat, I pushed my toes deep into golden, sugary sand. I didn't want the tops of my feet to scorch under the tropical sun.

I was on the North Shore of Oahu in Hawaii, lying side by side with Troy, my boyfriend and husband of thirty years. A dear friend had flown us here so that Troy, a licensed pastor, could officiate at the wedding of our friend's son and future bride. We were on a break from our wedding duties, savoring the beauty of Waimea Bay, one of the world's renowned surfing hubs. Because it was August, the world-class winter waves were long gone. In their place shimmered a sea of green glass.

Troy and I held hands and lounged in hammock-shaped holes we'd dug into the sand. We were like two bears hibernating out of season. I was sure that little—short of a tsunami siren—could convince me to haul my backside out of the comfortable and perfectly contoured sand chair I'd just created.

I was wrong, of course. The explorer's blood that courses through my veins has a very convincing voice. Regardless of where my ventures lead, I always feel the intrinsic draw to investigate the wild places around me. I've learned that every area has its own distinct features, its own unique beauty. During the many trips I've made to the Hawaiian Islands, I've swum a million miles with my head underwater. Exploring the intricate coastlands with a mask, snorkel, and fins is one of my favorite things on earth. By doing so, I've come to a conclusion: this world is just *amazing*!

What a God of wonders. We only need to look under the waves to see His vivid canvas filled with colorful diversity, texture, and design. When I'm snorkeling, my mind always bends toward the same question: why would God make an underwater world, which people would rarely see, so *astoundingly beautiful*? I'm convinced He did it simply because He can! He's an artist who instills profound splendor into every minute and grand thing He touches.

His artistry can be seen in the smallest wildflower petals and the highest glacier-sculpted peaks. His glory is crafted into the deepest hues of ocean blue and the broadest canyons and rivers. His awesome power is splashed across the vast purple blanket of stars overhead and captured in the intense color of a child's eyes. I believe He's created it all, in part, because He loves beauty.

Because of how deeply I feel the truths inspired by what I see, discovery of this remarkable world beckons my heart like the voice of a cherished friend. Even while resting, I hear the call.

As I was lying in the sun on Waimea Bay, I'd already scoped out the narrow vista between the brim of my hat and my chin. Within this one-inch panorama, I could see several rock structures beyond the mouth of the bay. Standing alone in the ocean only a few hundred yards away, they appeared to be all that remained of some ancient lava tubes. With rain clouds forming on the horizon, I knew this might be the last bit of brilliant sunlight we'd have to light our way. The call drew me like north pulls a compass needle. As enticing as my comfortable spot was, my inner explorer's voice was more so.

Sand was still firmly stuck to my back as I ducked under the waves to wet my hair. I slicked it back and strapped on my gear. Whether it brands me hard-core or not, this I know for certain: not once have I put my head under the sea and doubted whether it was completely worth it. For me, snorkeling is a wonder *every* time.

Troy, not wanting to miss out on an adventure, was soon by my side. Together we were immediately embraced by the cooling rush of fluid weightlessness. Swimming in suspended silence, with every stroke we drew deeper into a world beset with more color than the human eye can fully grasp. In the shallows we were hailed by a virtual rainbow of aquatic life. We streamed by schools of brilliant yellow tangs partially mixed with black-and-white sergeantfish. Nearly every nook featured finned bits of darting confetti. Each grotto staged a lively vignette of life under the sea.

As we ventured into deeper waters, the color and shape of life intensified into surreal combinations. Heavy parrotfish wore a delicious combination of sherbet colors. Moorish idols traced intricate patterns with their long trailing fins flowing like ribbons behind them.

Swimming in tandem, Troy and I skirted the outer fringe of a lava flow that dropped away in a rocky cascade of black boulders. All color deepened with the water. Simply looking downward revealed a visual feast of the richest blue.

Continuing to head toward the islets, we swam through what appeared to be bottomless waters. Doing so always makes me acutely aware of how small I am and how vulnerable I would be if approached by a predator. Hawaiian waters host a great variety of sharks that coexist peacefully with humans. Yet a few species, on rare occasions, will "taste" people. Of this menacing minority, the most deeply feared are tiger sharks. When these amazing predators—which can grow to twenty feet in length and are equipped with renewing rows of teeth—sample a human, the results are usually catastrophic.

I've seen several tigers. For me, their immense beauty is overshadowed by their chilling posture of pure menace. They can be as harmless as game fish, but just knowing they can bite a man in half inspires primal fear. I understand that nearly all encounters with sharks occur in shallow waters. Nevertheless, it's always the dark, deep waters that make my toes curl.

Seeing the flanks of the islets begin to materialize out of the heavy cobalt was both an ominous and welcome sight. The underwater landscape was dramatic, relating a history of fierce volcanic upheavals and violent collisions of molten lava with the sea.

Without warning, the brilliant folds of deep blue darkened into dismal, foreboding layers of dark gray. Unfortunately, my observation of the changing weather was correct. We were suddenly beset by a rollicking shower. We rounded the outside of the farthest lava dome, which was rimmed in pure blackness as the bottom plunged to depths beyond our comprehension. Together we began to cross the small distance between the two rocky zeniths.

At that moment, far beneath us in the darkness, a moving shadow caught my eye.

I reached out and squeezed Troy's hand. He quickly looked in the direction that I pointed. Immediately I felt him stiffen with alertness.

We hovered in the soft drone of pouring rain. The dark figure was moving directly below us and traveling in the same general direction. Slowly it began to rise out of the shadowy depths in a vague line in front of us.

I didn't realize I'd been holding my breath until I recognized the form and exhaled in a rush. It was only a green sea turtle!

Though I've swum with hundreds of turtles, each is still a special gift. I could see by the distinctively long, thick tail that this was a young male. The juvenile was surfacing for a breath of air. Turtles are usually shy, so I thought it strange that this one seemed unaware of our proximity. As he drew closer, I saw why. He didn't see us. The truth was, he *couldn't*.

When the turtle came more fully into view, deep sorrow gripped my heart. An enormous tangle of fishing line was wrapped around his head and front flippers. An additional wad trailed from this mass, under his carapace and out into silver lines a half-dozen feet behind him. Snarled among the heavy lines were the remnants of several dilapidated foam floats. One was tightly knotted between his right eye and right flipper. Perhaps because of repeated contact with the float, his right eye was completely white and unseeing.

There was more. The turtle was also afflicted with numerous tumors, some the size of softballs around the areas where the fishing line had contact with his skin. It appeared this beleaguered little guy had been carrying his burden for quite some time. The lines on either side of his head had sawed down nearly two inches into his flesh. These areas were white with what I assumed was infection.

Held motionless by sorrow, I watched him surface not six feet away from me. Even though every movement must have been painful, he was still trying to live. With his small snout lifted high in the falling rain, he drew in one deep breath after another.

My mind filled with questions. *Why, God? In the vast Pacific, on this day, in this place, at this exact moment, why would You guide this dying turtle to me? What can I do? What can I learn? What can I—*My thoughts were cut short by near-electric realization. Suddenly I knew I was in this place, at this time, with this turtle, for one reason—*to save it.*

Here, near the surface and away from the protection of hiding places in the coral far below, the turtle was vulnerable. He would remain close by for only a few minutes, if not seconds. I didn't have much time.

Usually turtles will tolerate humans in their proximity only if there's no overt or aggressive move toward them. Because the turtle had rotated to view us with his seeing eye, he knew we were there. Somehow I would have to casually swim closer to the turtle long enough for him not to view my presence as a threat. In a very short time, I needed to show him I wasn't interested in harming him.

I told Troy of my plans and asked for his help. He agreed to gently block the opposite side of the turtle to keep him circling as long as possible. By doing so, we all slowly swam together. Though I was on his blind side, the young turtle knew I was with him. He swung his ailing head in small circles, trying to locate exactly where I was. After several moments he seemed convinced I was not going to hurt him and allowed me to move closer.

I knew I would get only one chance to free this little guy, and I needed to make sure I was in the best possible position. We were running out of time. The turtle swung his head away from me. He was already beginning his slow descent back into the depths. This was it.

I darted in and grabbed the trailing line under his carapace and wrapped it twice around my hand. The turtle felt the line pull deeper into his flesh and instinctively dove straight down, taking me with him.

Together we plunged headfirst toward blackness. My ears popped repeatedly as the gray light from the surface rapidly dimmed. Unable to reach his head as he plummeted, in a final effort I yanked as hard as I could and felt a snap.

Kicking back toward the surface, I looked at the line I'd pulled free. It was only a portion of what I knew was still snarled around the turtle. For all my good intention and effort, what I'd done hadn't helped the turtle at all. I looked down in mounting grief as the dying turtle dove deeper into the inky water from which he had come.

My frustration rose with my tears. I had failed. A dying soul needed my help, and the best I could do was cause it more pain.

Again I questioned: *Why, God? In Your world so full of beauty, how does this senseless tragedy fit? What am I supposed to learn from this?*

The rain, which had fallen softly earlier, now came down so hard that the surface of the sea appeared to boil. It seemed that even the sky was crying for this doomed turtle. The firmament appeared even more gray. My attention alternated between the fishing line still in my hand and the black abyss into which the turtle had plunged.

With rain spattering on my head, the voice of the Lord began to gently fill my heart: *Look at this consuming blackness, My child, and never forget. This is—exactly—what it looks like when you allow yourself to become entangled in sin. You become snared and infected, blinded by all you choose to value over Me.*

In moments of despair you call on My Name…and I come. Releasing you from your bondage can be painful, especially the longer you let the bonds grow into your flesh. When I try to tear your entrapments away, you have a choice. You can be still and know that I am your God. You can patiently allow Me to free you, to heal you. Or you can turn away from Me toward your own understanding and, just like this turtle, plunge into utter darkness, toward your own destruction.

This is what it looks like when you turn away from Me and try to solve your own problems.

Remember.

Remember.

I've kept a fragment of that fishing line to this day.

Time to Stop Running

The more we run from the Lord, the more we become entangled in the traps of the enemy. We have but one escape—to stop running away and start running toward the welcoming arms of a loving God.

Sins—even "little" ones—have a way of turning into something terrible. They're not content to stay in the corner where we believe we've confined them. Instead, our hoarded indulgences will mimic the invasive behavior of an abandoned kudzu vine. Left unattended, they send up growing tendrils that invade every area of our souls. Like any parasite they multiply at an alarming rate. Our sins wrap and curl a black, threadlike network around every thought and deed, stealing away our lives as they go. What's certain about this insidious tangle of death is that it will *never* stop growing.

Most of us have experienced moments of feeling surrounded by the negative things we've permitted to enter our lives. Among these threads of destruction, we become like a hapless butterfly landing within a web. We believe the silvery filaments that surround us are no match for our ability to fly away. Yet moment by moment, day by day, season by season, the sheer number of these evil, multiplying strands subtly, silently overwhelms our capability to extricate our hearts from their consuming grasp. Without rescue, a grim fate awaits.

It's easy for us to feel trapped and helpless against the negative things we've opened our lives to. But there *is* something we can do.

Freedom begins with a single decision.

No knot of sin can withstand a repentant heart that honestly cries out to Jesus. No matter how we became ensnared or how confusing our entrapment might be, there is no bond of darkness that the redeeming love of Jesus cannot cut through.

Yet we must realize something first. The real truth about our bondage is this: the things that cause so much havoc in our lives *don't* actually hold us. *We hold them!*

Think about it. God's Word is clear. He repeatedly warns us to be careful of the things we enjoy so they don't grow into habits that control us: "Even though 'I am allowed to do anything,' I must not become a slave to anything" (1 Corinthians 6:12). Sadly, the overriding voice of this world calls us to reject any sort of control as an infringement on our right to have fun. Many of us believe that real freedom is doing anything we want. The truth is that when we follow our every sensual desire and a soft life of pleasure, we eventually become a slave to them.

Unlike the turtle, we're not helpless in escaping from what binds us. Often it's something we're choosing *not* to escape from. Because God sent His Son to free the lost, from His perspective we are holding our shackles in one hand and the keys to freedom in Christ in the other. The real question is, which do we love more—our freedom in Christ or our bondage to sin?

Choosing to let go of sin and embrace Christ is only the first step. Like the helpless turtle that couldn't escape the tangle of fishing line and floats, we are equally helpless to cause our sin to go away. If we truly want to be released from our pain, we must make the decision to stop bolting away from God once we've asked for His help. The removal of things that have grown into our flesh can be painful, but leaving them to fester in our souls can be fatal.

We must make the decision to be still, to stay with our Rescuer through the pain and allow Him to carefully extricate every strand of darkness.

This process reminds me of training horses in our round pen. Some of the horses that come to our ranch have little or no experience with humans. Because they view people as predators, when placed in a round corral, they will run in circles, looking for a way of escape. Some canter lap after lap around me, driven by their fear, desire for dominance, or pride.

No matter what motivates a horse's flight from me, my first goal is to encourage it to slow down and trust me enough to stop running. Through subtle cues I help the horse understand that the best thing to do is stand still, turn to face me, and look at me with both eyes.

Once I've gained the horse's trust and full attention, the foundation of our relationship is built on his choice to *come* to me. The horse must choose to walk into the center of the circle and stand with me. It's here that the horse finds rest, peace, and love. The horse is free of any restraints and can bolt anytime it wants. But if it runs away, there will be no rest. The horse must keep moving its feet until it chooses to return. As long as the horse continues to run, it gains no freedom.

When the horse finally makes the choice to stop running—to come to me and stand still at my side—the healing of its brokenness begins. For it is only when it chooses to stand with me that I am able to gently place my hands over every part of its body. By doing so, I put all doubt about me to rest, and the horse is able to physically feel my gift of love and peace.

Are you held captive by sin wrapped around your heart? No matter how badly trapped you've become and how strongly you desire to bolt, you have a Rescuer. His name is Jesus. In the presence of His love, peace, and rest, no shackle can survive.

Will you choose to hold still and allow the One who made you...*to free you*?

6

THE WOUND

Our One Hope

While relocating a horse in need, some of my staff became aware of two dogs that lived in the same crumbling location. Among their other visible problems, both dogs had been starved to half their normal body weight. Kelsie and Laurie decided after much prayer and consideration that they could do more than simply feel bad—they could each make a difference for a dog in need. They returned to the dilapidated residence, and each brought home one of the suffering canines.

Immediately a sad truth emerged. For these rescued dogs, being savagely thin was not their worst problem. Laurie's dog had a severe and potentially lethal form of diabetes, and Kelsie's dog had a very serious injury to her throat.

The dog Kelsie chose, a Dalmatian mix, was sweet and mostly white with an adorable black patch over one eye. On the day of her rescue, the dog was so ill that Kelsie drove her directly to a veterinary hospital.

At the clinic the doctor determined that the injured dog was feverish from a systemic infection. He also examined the gash on her neck—a gruesome, gaping three-by-five-inch hole in her throat just below her chin. From the wound seeped a continuous issue of bloody serum and pus. Kelsie was sent home with a sack brimming with powerful antibiotics and detailed instructions on how to administer aid to her new, sick dog.

On the way home Kelsie reached across to the passenger seat, where her ailing dog lay curled. She gently stroked the wounded animal's head to comfort her. The feeble dog lifted only her eyes, apparently too weak to move much else. In the moments that followed, Kelsie's car slowly began to fill with the soft, continuous rhythm of canine gratitude. In glances as she drove, Kelsie watched hope begin to rise within the dog's ravaged body. In a feeble effort at thankfulness, her tail gently strummed against the seat. And so a new friendship began.

A week later at the ranch, with a radiant smile, Kelsie announced, "Her name is Dakota. It's a Native American word for 'friend.'" Dakota's new moniker instantly became a purposeful banner over her life. Even in her weakness during her recovery, she was indeed a friend to all. Seasoned with multiple veterinary appointments, Dakota's health slowly began to rally.

Initially her front legs appeared to be extremely weak and uncoordinated. Unlike a healthy dog, she could not reach forward to hop up a step or spring over an obstacle. I also noticed that she relaxed in a peculiar position. Dakota consistently held her left front leg and shoulder slightly elevated and pulled in toward her center. In this stance she turned her head slightly to the left, with her chin tucked down toward her body. This was not a normal posture for a resting dog.

Another strange observation was that she was terrified when others were motionless and intently focused on her. I noticed this the first time I tried to steady myself to take her picture. She was content and seemed to enjoy the attention I gave her until I pulled out my camera and turned it in her direction. Her response was to run and hide under the nearest truck. Kelsie and I were left to look at each other and ponder the reason for this peculiar behavior.

Despite her mysterious conduct, Dakota slowly gained weight and strength. She began to run and play with other dogs and eventually became a beloved friend to Seven, my small blue heeler.

Kelsie was told that in this stage of Dakota's recovery, exercise would be good for her dog. The vet shared that it would stimulate her circulation, muscle development, and general well-being. When asked about the possibility of taking Dakota on a pack trip, the vet said it would be a fine idea.

After discussing it thoroughly, Kelsie and I agreed on a plan of action. Because we always hike in while leading our horses under panniers, we knew if Dakota became fatigued, we could easily boost her onto one of their five strong backs.

Once our horses were packed with enough gear and food for nearly a week, we cinched each of their loads into a high and tight position. After performing a quick check of every buckle, strap, and knot, we joined hands to pray over the trip. With all of us carrying our own backpacks and guiding our own horses, we set off toward a new adventure.

Our travels would take us approximately seven miles into the Cascade wilderness. Since we're constantly training our horses, I wanted each one to experience every position, from leader to follower, along the trail. To accomplish this, we rotated horse and hiker teams every thirty minutes. While guiding Cade—a relatively new-to-us, smoky buckskin— in the front of the string, I took great pleasure in observing how much Dakota enjoyed simply being a dog.

She and Seven, or Sevi for short, explored every bush, log, and tree. Once we broke out of the forest onto the high Wickiup Plains, the two dogs ran with complete abandon, bumping shoulders as their canine teeth clashed in an open-mouthed romp of blatant joy. Had they let loose with a life-is-awesome celebration howl, I certainly would've joined them. Just the thought of it made me smile. It was wonderful to see this sweet dog getting better physically and feeling better too.

After nearly two hours of hiking along the abrupt edge of an immense obsidian lava flow that soared three hundred feet above us, high plains gave way to a sweeping north-slope descent into a glorious, old growth forest. The snowcapped panorama of the pumice plains quietly succumbed to the towering, cool depths of the mossy canopy above. Snow-fed streams tumbled all around us, each flanked by a brilliant tapestry of pink monkey flowers, purple larkspur, red Indian paintbrush, and orange columbine. Small yellow flowers that I didn't recognize also seemed to join in the merriment with a bright, visual laughter of their own. After another hour we turned off the main trail and blazed to what I knew in my heart to be nearly hallowed ground.

The dense forest opened up into an expansive, southern-sloping meadow. While striding through the knee-deep grass, I realized this massive, green wonderland was also a favorite banquet area for mule deer, elk, and bears, as well as the steed at my side. The look of pure awe on my horse's face was priceless. Perhaps he believed that somewhere along the way he had crossed an invisible threshold and had been transported from earth directly into heaven itself.

We set up our base camp away from the meadow in a dense stand of trees. Because the thick canopy overhead thwarted any fragile plants or underbrush from growing beneath them, it was an ideal place to camp with minimum impact.

Each day held unique rewards. Heralding every morning was a glorious sunrise, a visual concert with golden spears of light pouring over the jagged eastern horizon. On horseback we navigated by compass and daily indulged in hillsides of blueberries warmed by the sun. We exchanged all reason for the pure "wahoo" factor of plunging into a frigid lake. Evenings were framed by soft facial expressions warmed by the amber glow of a fire. And a grand finale came while lying on our backs in the meadow at night and watching our breath rise beneath a glittering display of endless stars.

Within the vast array of gifts that our days held, there was one consistent task that Kelsie faithfully performed. Each morning and evening she heated water over the fire and made hot poultices to help draw out the seeping infection that still plagued Dakota's wounded throat. In an attempt to keep the gash as clean as possible, after each hot-pack application, Kelsie tied a fresh handkerchief around the area where a collar would normally be.

Despite Kelsie's continuing treatments, the wound on Dakota's neck simply would not heal.

After our arrival home, my thoughts again turned toward Kelsie's new companion. To the best of our knowledge, it had been a full four months since Dakota's initial injury. The former owners had told Kelsie they believed the dog had been attacked by a bobcat. While neither of us believed that was the real story, we conceded that it didn't matter how she was injured, only that her wound was not healing. After more trips to the vet than Kels could count on her hands, dozens of poultice applications, wound ointments, three full rounds of powerful antibiotics, and plenty of rest and exercise, Dakota's throat injury persisted. Though she had returned to a normal weight and her wound was vastly improved, what troubled me most was that it was still festering.

Kelsie and I now believed the wound track in Dakota's neck traveled downward. This meant that any infection or minor debris would travel deeper into her body instead of flowing out. I shared Kelsie's gut feeling that *something* was still inside Dakota, something her body could not expel.

At the veterinary hospital we explained our suspicions to Dr. Shawn, a new veterinarian who hadn't yet seen Dakota. He agreed there might be a fragment of some foreign body that had pushed down into the wound, perhaps a sliver of wood or even a piece of cheat grass. Either way, he was going to shoot a few x-rays before he surgically cleansed the seeping gash. It was his opinion this would take care of Dakota's problem once and for all.

Pushing through the exit doorway of the hospital and walking out with Kels to my truck—without Dakota—was hard. Barely settled into the passenger seat, my dear friend yielded to the pressure of her building tears. In a voice filled with emotion, Kelsie explained how much she loved this special dog and how—true to her name—she had become one of her dearest and closest friends. Flooded by another tearful tide, she barely managed to express that she didn't know how she would make it...if Dakota didn't survive.

Teardrops slipped off Kelsie's chin and dotted the front of her green ranch shirt. I reached across the cab of my truck and took her hands, and together we prayed.

Fortified with the information that Dr. Shawn would call with an update as soon as Dakota was out of surgery, we made our way back to Crystal Peaks and prepared for the upcoming day.

As always, the ranch was bursting with activity. Kelsie was bright, giving all she had to the kids and families she worked with. Yet knowing my good friend so well, I could sense her deep concern even from a distance.

Late in the afternoon Kelsie bolted toward me—cell phone in hand—across the ranch's main yard. Even before she spoke, I could see by her expression that she was equally elated and amazed. Her words poured out in an excited jumble of relief and astonishment.

Sarah, my friend who as a young girl had helped me build the ranch, was now a veterinary technician working with Dr. Shawn. She'd just called and explained to Kelsie how she was routinely bringing the x-rays up on a computer screen in their darkroom before Dakota's surgery. Sarah explained that when she realized *what* she was seeing, an electric surge rose from the soles of her feet and exited the back of her neck, jolting her thick, blond hair into needling hackles.

On the x-rays, materializing out of the darkness like a milky phantom, was an image of pure evil. Finally the source of Dakota's four months of continuous suffering was fully revealed. Having passed through the dog's throat and beneath her shoulder blade, the lethal intruder was wedged against her spine. It was *an arrow*!

The triple-bladed razors of a two-inch stainless-steel broadhead floated into view, with an eight-inch section of graphite shaft *still* attached. The projectile lodged within her body was *ten inches long*. The protruding remnants of the shaft did not exhibit the splintering break of an accident. It was obvious that the arrow's shaft had been intentionally and cleanly cut with a smooth edge just below the surface of Dakota's throat. Someone somewhere had done this on purpose and then tried to hide the deed.

Yet what confounded us the most was that Dakota was able to

maintain the life of a normal dog with a nearly foot-long, razor-sharp weapon buried deep inside her chest.

How was it possible that she lived at all?

Because the arrow had miraculously passed through Dakota's neck without severing any vital structures, Dr. Shawn knew it would be far too dangerous to try to retrieve the razored projectile the same way it entered. Instead, he opted to remove it dorsally through a large incision that he carefully made on her back. Once the arrow was extricated, Dakota made a complete and nearly instant recovery.

In no time she was bounding around the property. One evening while preparing for a ranch fellowship, I watched her as she bounced in delight, a knotted rope toy in her mouth. She had just stolen the treasure from a group of small boys who now chased after her with squealing abandon. From then on it was always easy to find Kelsie on the ranch. One only needed to follow the white dog with the charming black patch over her eye.

I look at that arrow, propped up in a green, enameled cup in my office, nearly every day. Sometimes when I'm on the phone, I pick it up and slowly spin it between my thumb and index finger. Without fail, I'm awed and a bit sickened by the horrifying destruction that three spinning razor blades can exact. I don't wish to forget what this weapon looks like or stop imagining how it might feel if it were sunk into *my* chest.

When I look at the arrow, I also remember something else—how a dog, a wonderful creation considered to be man's best friend, had survived the worst humans had to offer, was found, and was saved by the unexpected and persistent love of a stranger.

FROM DARKNESS TO LIGHT

We can be so ashamed of some sins that
we push them down deep inside. Beyond
the view of others, these are the sins that kill.

We've all made mistakes, and we've all said and done things we're not proud of. Some of these choices can be devastating—an abortion, an affair, a betrayal. In some cases our missteps bring so much pain and shame that we push them down into our hearts and turn them into secrets. We bury them like old bones, hoping to plant them so deep that no one will ever find them.

The problem with hidden sins, however, is that they don't ever go away. Sooner or later these sins *will* ruin us. Attempting to conceal a sin is no less harmful than choosing to ram an arrow of selfish rebellion into our own chests. Once the infection sets in, it festers and spreads, eventually leading to our destruction.

We all know that covering up our problems won't solve them. Neither will attempting to bury them under an avalanche of feel-good procedures, treatments, and programs. We can't heal our sin on the inside by simply looking better on the outside. No external polishing can cure an internal rot.

There's no regime of eating right, healthy living, or exercise habits that will make the damage from our sin cease. There's no combination of righteous living, volunteering, mission trips, or good deeds that can stave off its evil seep. There's no medication on earth that can cure it. There's no amount of sex, drinking, or drugs that can mask its effects. There's no distraction in fantasy books, movies, romance novels, video games, texting, Facebook messaging, tweeting, blogging, or online chatting that can negate sin's presence in our lives. There's no amount of cutting, burning, tattooing, piercing, binging, purging, or starving that can camouflage the pain we feel inside.

If you feel as if you're reading about yourself in Dakota's story—pierced, broken, with an arrow of sin in your life that you can't remove—know that there is a remedy. There is *one* hope.

God's Word says, "Oh, what a miserable person I am! Who will free me from this life that is dominated by sin? Thank God! The answer is in Jesus Christ our Lord" (Romans 7:24–25).

If you feel alone in your pain or pride, realize that you're not. Scripture tells us, "For all have sinned; all fall short of God's glorious standard. Yet now God in his gracious kindness declares us not guilty. He has done this through Christ Jesus, who has freed us by taking away our sins" (Romans 3:23–24). We all can be saved in this same way, no matter who we are or what we have done.

Perhaps David said it best in one of his most beloved psalms: "I prayed to the LORD, and he answered me, freeing me from *all* my fears.... The LORD hears his people when they call to him for help. He rescues them from *all* their troubles. The LORD is close to the brokenhearted; he rescues those who are crushed in spirit" (34:4, 17–18). "Those who look to him for help will be radiant with joy; no shadow of shame will darken their faces. In my desperation I prayed, and the LORD listened; he saved me from *all* my troubles" (verses 5–6, NLT, 2007).

The healing truth of God's Word declares that "anyone who calls on the name of the Lord will be saved" and "If we confess our sins to him, he is faithful and just to forgive us and to cleanse us from every wrong" (Romans 10:13; 1 John 1:9). If you feel pierced, there is One who wants to give you forgiveness, cleansing, and redemption… All you need to do is fall on your knees and ask.

Friend, there is *no* arrow that the unfailing love of Jesus cannot remove.

Editor's Note: Read more about Kelsie in the story "A Perfect Match," found in Kim's book *Hope Rising;* about Laurie and her dog Mia in Kim's book *Blind Hope;* and about Sarah in the story "Run Through Fire" in *Hope Rising.*

7

THE ATTACK

Fierce Defense

I love my ranch staff. They're some of my dearest friends, and I consider them my family. Because they hail from across the United States, I'm passionate about introducing them to the marvels of this wild, western world. It's my delight to take them back-country skiing, surfing, mountaineering, horse packing, rock climbing, night snowshoeing, marathon running, snorkeling, and various other forms of adventuring and exploring.

Of all the precious gems the Northwest has to offer, perhaps the most extraordinary is Yellowstone National Park. If you'd like to discover our God of wonders in a no-words-can-describe way, Yellowstone is a must-see. I'm certain the word *amazing* was coined there.

Because it gives me great joy to share my passions with those I love, a handful of my staff and I decided to do a whirlwind trip to this Serengeti of North America. Since it was September and our ranch season was still in full swing, we needed to make the trip as quickly as possible. This meant we would blitz the twelve-hour drive in one day, have two full days in the park, and then bolt home again. Taking in the whole park in two days is simply not possible, but jet-propelled by a ton of coffee, we were determined to try!

Our plan was to spend the first day viewing as much geothermal activity as we could squeeze in. The second day would be devoted to seeing as many animals as we could locate between dawn and dusk.

I've visited Yellowstone during many different seasons, and it *never* disappoints. My girls' initial wide-eyed responses confirmed that this trip would be no exception. After a full day of viewing all the massive geysers, steaming ponds, burbling mud pots, and exquisitely colored pools that we could mash in between sunup and sundown, we bundled up and fell into our sleeping bags. Like expectant treasure hunters, we vowed to rise early with the wildlife the following day in hopes of seeing something incredible.

The next morning we woke up to the high-country phenomenon known as "tent snow." It was so cold during the night that our respiration froze into thin white sheets of ice that clung perilously to the *inside* of our tents. After pausing only long enough to brew some joe, we filled our travel mugs to the brim and set off. My truck was loaded with five girls; four more rode in another car behind us. I thrust my small camera out the window, wordlessly asking everyone in the car behind me if they had theirs handy. Four little thumbs shot up enthusiastically.

With hands full of coffee and cameras, we were good to go. To fan the fires of anticipation, I tossed a question to the girls in my truck: "If you could see *any* animal that lives in this park, which would you choose?"

Kelsie, who sat next to me in the center of the front seat, immediately answered with a monstrous grin, "If I saw a bear, I'd be so excited that I just might pee in my pants!" Laughter erupted when I told her to move to the backseat so I wouldn't have to share in that experience.

While winding our way up 8,859-foot Dunraven Pass, we rounded a turn on a particularly steep slope and were surprised by a traffic jam. Of course, that's Yellowstone language for "Stop here! There's something fun to see!" As we carefully threaded our way through the bottleneck of parked cars and people milling about to find the best view, I asked some folks what was causing all the commotion. One pointed nearly straight up toward the ridge above us and said, "There's a *grizzly bear*!" Upon hearing those words, Kelsie nearly leaped out the window like a dog after a Frisbee. Lucky for me, she did *not* make good on her earlier promise, and we both exited the truck with dry jeans.

Sure enough, approximately one hundred yards up the mountainside was a subadult grizzly. The bruin appeared to be taking great joy in climbing up small pine trees, breaking the entire top off, and then raiding the pine cones for nuts. The delight I took in watching the bear was completely eclipsed by the deep satisfaction of watching *Kelsie* watch the bear. My friend's feet scarcely touched the ground. After the bear ambled out of sight and everyone loaded back into the truck, voices excitedly overlapped as five girls talked at once about the thrill of seeing a Yellowstone grizzly.

A quarter mile up the road we came upon another traffic jam. This time it was caused by a mother black bear with two small cubs. Because she had taken her youngsters below the road into thick underbrush, the mother bear and her family were more difficult to watch. Yet it was still a thrill to see flashes of jet black among the deep green forest. Several times the cubs rolled into view as they wrestled and played around their mother. They seemed oblivious to the ecstatic commotion that their presence aroused in all who witnessed them. Again we piled back into the truck. Kelsie looked at me with a grin that barely fit on her face. "I could go home right now!" she said. "Already this has been so amazing!"

As our day rolled on, it seemed around every turn the Lord blessed us with something incredible to behold. We viewed waterfalls so delicate they fell like angel's breath, while others roared with enough power to shake the earth. Our little caravan came across deer, antelope, and elk napping in the sun. Herds of bison moved like slow, black rivers through the valleys and occasionally washed over the roadways in front of us, creating delightful traffic jams of their own.

About midday the other carload of girls decided they wanted to detour into the town of West Yellowstone to warm up and walk through some of the artisan shops. With parting hugs we sent them on their way and continued our exploration of all things inside the borders of the park.

We paused in the small town of Mammoth to stretch our legs. While there, we discovered that each grassy area between the buildings boasted groups of grazing elk. As we viewed a particularly massive male, a ranger told us we were fortunate to be witnessing the largest bull elk in the park. We'd just missed seeing him defend his herd against an unfortunate suitor who was sulking nearby.

He was unquestionably the most massive bull I'd ever seen. He seemed to revel in the fact that we were so taken by him. After strutting across the road right in front of us, he displayed his power by lowering his enormous antlers to the ground, violently swinging his head from side to side, and destroying everything in his path. Huge chunks of grass filled the air as he physically demonstrated to all other bulls, "Guys, you don't want *any* of this!"

After a bit of hiking around Mammoth Hot Springs, we arrived at Willow Park just as dusk approached. Perhaps because we had seen so many spectacular sights already, we were certain that any minute a moose would roam into view.

Willow Park is a riparian area approximately two miles long. It runs parallel to and slightly lower than the road we drove on. The "park" is basically a high, narrow meadow with streams meandering through its length. Since willow thrives particularly well here, so does a healthy moose population.

After completing several mooseless passes, we stopped at all the turn-outs and scrutinized each brown stream bank, log, and stump. We were sure that every distant, dark form had the potential to be a moose sighting. Thankfully, the park was empty of cars, so we were able to continue our inspection at about five miles an hour. At one point we even pulled off, and two of the girls hopped out in hopes of taking a game trail that descended to the creek in order to get a closer look at what might be coming to drink.

As the girls started into the tall willows, I felt a strong warning to call them back to the safety of our vehicle. The animals in Yellowstone are large and wild. Surprising them on a narrow game trail at dusk would not be a good idea.

To oblige my mother-bear instincts, the girls loaded back into the truck in the same order they'd ridden all day. Kelsie slid into the front seat beside me with Laurie next to her and the passenger door. Not wanting to miss any action by stopping for dinner, we opted instead for a ritual ranch tradition—we raided whatever we could find under the seats. As buried snacks emerged, so did the jokes about who was willing to eat what and how long it'd been down there.

I'm still the reigning diner when it comes to eating dodgy, found-under-the-seat cuisine. I managed to find a petrified pack of red licorice, while Kels and Laurie located a more nutritious offering of string cheese and crackers. Kelsie grabbed a handful and sent the rest into the backseat. Then she transformed into a cheese-eating machine.

Just as I was about to warn her not to mistakenly bite my arm, a flash of movement caught my eye. To my astonishment two grizzly cubs galloped across the road just thirty feet in front of us!

I was so excited I couldn't get any words out. The best I could manage was to stammer, point, and finally shout, "Bears!"

The cubs were not ambling or trotting. They were running as fast as little bears could go. They darted across the pavement, scaled an eight-foot embankment on our left, and began bounding up a very steep hill. To get a better view, I quickly rolled the truck up the road to the exact location where they'd crossed in front of us.

Then, before I could watch the babies, *Mom* galloped out of the brush with a third cub on her heels. She was so close she nearly brushed the front of our truck. Her sheer size left me incredulous. The bear's body was larger than some of the smaller horses on our ranch. Yet, despite her mass and power, her ears were down in a submissive position. Something had threatened these bears enough to make them believe they were in mortal danger. The mother was clearly hustling her family to safety. I watched the muscles of her back and shoulders ripple under her thick, glossy pelt. She was beautiful!

Still at a dead run, she looked over her shoulder once and then, in a single leap, jumped up the same embankment her two cubs had just climbed and continued sprinting up the hill with the third cub in tow. I watched in slack-jawed awe as she bounded up the steep ridge.

Everything seemed to happen fast and slow at the same time. I grabbed my camera, turned it on, and waited to activate the telephoto lens. The mother bear was about thirty yards up the hillside when I framed her up.

Through the lens of my camera, as if I were viewing a *National Geographic* moment, I watched the scene. Without warning, the mother bear planted her left hind foot. In a single motion her body whirled around like a great, dark cape.

She didn't miss a beat. Instead of watching her hind legs launch up the hill, I was now seeing her front legs charge down the hill. In a series of great leaps, she stormed directly toward us. My *National Geographic* picture suddenly turned into a horror scene.

Inside the truck I dropped my camera. The elation the girls and I had felt milliseconds earlier instantly transformed into terror.

In one last vault the mother bear landed squarely on the top of the embankment only four yards from our truck! She was slightly higher than my driver's side window and could easily jump across. We were now eye to eye!

What I saw next is permanently seared into my memory. As the mother bear's front paws hit the top of the embankment, her momentum forced her weight toward us. In an effort to keep from tumbling over the bank and into the truck, she drove all her claws forward and down, exposing their full length. In the same instant, her ears pressed backward, flat against her head, as all the hair down her back stood straight up. In one final display of fury, she pulled her lips back as far as possible and let out a fearsome, teeth-clenched, growl! The sound was loud enough for me to hear above the rumble of my truck's engine.

In a fraction of a second, this bear showed me *every* weapon she had. In all my life I'd never seen an image of greater ferocity. Her message was obvious: "These are *my* cubs, and this is *my* territory, and if you don't leave *now*...I *will* kill you!" She was so close that I could clearly see—and in my mind I *still* do—how perfectly her bared teeth fit together.

In what seemed like slow motion, I watched the bear bring her hind legs forward and begin to coil her body like a spring. Clearly, the mother grizzly's next intention was to jump the short distance into my open truck window!

That was the exact moment when the electrical connection between my brain and right foot finally fired. It was the closest I've ever come to discovering if my Dodge Dually could pop a wheelie!

With cheese and body parts flying, we careened down the road a quarter mile before pulling off to gather ourselves. Since we'd all been watching the charging grizzly on our left, I hadn't realized Laurie had leaned out the open passenger window and was looking over the top of the cab to get a better picture. Although she had a firm grasp on the safety handle, when I gunned the truck, she almost did the splits to maintain her balance.

Kelsie, meanwhile, had imitated a cartoon Tasmanian devil and nearly spun a hole in the seat next to me. When she finally stopped turning, she was upside down and face up with her head under the dashboard. At one point during our flight, either her knee or foot smashed against my throat—I'm still not sure which. Adding to our disarray were fragments of cheese and crackers everywhere.

After righting both Kelsie and Laurie, picking strands of cheese out of my hair, and doing a quick head count (surprisingly, I could still count to five), everyone burst out in an uncontrollable rush of adrenalized laughter. Had our words been racehorses, they would have been heading down the homestretch. With everyone jabbering at once, it was my extrapolation that Kelsie had spun around in the seat about eight times before going headfirst under the dash. None of us was completely sure why, but we thought she was trying to hit the gas pedal with her hands!

Our conclusion was that *no one* gets to see what we had just seen… and live.

While we continued to mop up inside the cab, a small blue truck pulled to a stop next to us. The driver rolled down his window and blithely drawled, "You guys seen anything?" Clearly, he was not prepared for the onslaught of nearly hysterical words that poured from our truck into his. As our story unfolded, he glanced knowingly at another man seated in the truck with him. Once we finished, he stared at me for a long moment. Finally he said, "Well, I'd say you got lucky. A ranger told me earlier today that more'n likely this same bear, a sow with three cubs, full-on attacked a car this morning."

Again I envisioned the perfectly fit teeth, grimacing only a few yards from my face. We were more than lucky—much more. The Lord had allowed us to experience something amazing, something incredible, something threatening…for a reason. We would *never* forget it.

Defending Our Hearts

> Are we as ferocious as a mother grizzly
> in our determination to drive sin out of
> our lives?

The day after our encounter with the mama grizzly at Yellowstone, the girls and I had a twelve-hour drive home to discuss what had happened. We took the time to fully enjoy the fact that God has an uproarious sense of humor. We tried to imagine God saying something like, "Hey, girls! If you think watching a grizzly bear run up a hill is cool, wait till you see *this*!"

Finally, when our laughter quieted into a more serious dialogue, I asked, "Why do you think the Lord allowed us to be charged by a bear? What do you think He wants us to learn from seeing something so remarkable?"

In moments such as these, I might be the leader of events and discussions, but I'm also the student. I'm convinced that I'm far more blessed by the wisdom of these young women than the other way around. Thoughtfully they began to explore my questions. As always, I was amazed by the varied truths each shared. All offered their views except one. I glanced in the rearview mirror and saw Jenna, my shy girl, staring out the window. The cab fell silent.

Jenna blinked her beautiful blue eyes a few times. I smiled, realizing that horses do exactly the same thing when they're thinking. In what I've come to love as her trademark quiet voice, she said, "Even though I wasn't in the truck with you guys when this happened, I know what this represents to me. I want to be just like that grizzly. I want to be just as ferocious as a charging bear toward *anything* that comes between me and God. I don't want to tolerate *any* sin, even the little ones that seem harmless. I want to drive them all out."

The rest of us sat in silence and let the powerful weight of her words sink in.

Jenna's answer triggered a thought.

I've often contemplated the actions of the religious leaders back in the apostles' day. Repeatedly, when these civic leaders were confronted with the truth of Christ, they came up with some excuse to drive great men of faith and the truth they carried as far away as they could. Instead of embracing hope in Christ, they pushed it away. With this in mind, perhaps one of the wisest questions we can ask ourselves is, on this day *am I?*

Am I behaving like the religious leaders of old, driving away the truth of Jesus and replacing it with my excuses, my desires, my self-justifications? The honest answer for each of us can be found by simply looking at *what* we're driving out of our hearts: our sin…or our Savior?

We cannot run toward and away from God at the same time.

It is our actions, words, and thoughts that prove what is true. If these things point toward serving ourselves, how do we make it right? How do we realistically chase sin out of our lives?

Well, light and darkness cannot live in the same place.

The answer, then, is simple: we must first recognize our sin. This is necessary because we will not fight that which we do not acknowledge exists. Once we've identified our sin and darkness, we need to drive them out by inviting our Lord to transform and cleanse our minds. He does this by pouring His redeeming light of truth into our lives.

Romans 12:2 states, "Don't copy the behavior and customs of this world, but let God *transform* you into a new person by changing the way you think. Then you will *know* what God wants you to do, and you will *know* how good and pleasing and perfect his will really is."

Plainly stated, we force sin out of our lives by driving the truth of God's Word in. How? The same way we drive anything into our lives—through repetition. We do this by purposefully choosing to follow Jesus' Word and just as purposely choosing to release our own desires. God's truth will become part of our lives when we *make* it a part by spending time in His Word every day.

Equally important is setting aside time to pray. Prayer is a vital connection between God and us. It changes everything in our lives. Because it changes our very foundations, it changes our hearts. When our foundations are strong, everything we build on top of them is strong as well. A simple reflection of this truth is how difficult it is to maintain ill feelings toward others when we purpose in our hearts to *consistently* pray for them. They may or may not change…but *we* do.

Remember, light and darkness cannot share the same territory.

On that long drive from Yellowstone, Jenna's soft voice echoed my thoughts when she asked herself a single question: "Within the territory of my heart, am I choosing to tolerate sin, or am I fiercely defending the heart Jesus Christ gave His life to set free?"

Friend, how would you answer?

THE KING

8

THE WOMAN

A Crown and a Sword

On a late summer evening, the last fiery slivers of sunlight splayed between the craggy peaks of the Cascade mountains. I was working in my lookout, a small room perched on ten-foot stilts, located on the highest crest of our ranch. From this special refuge I took a few moments to admire the saw-toothed beauty of the mountains and reflect on the dream I'd had a few weeks before—the eagle that refused to leave its gilded prison because it was more concerned with appearance and ease than with true freedom.

I wondered, *Am I somehow like this majestic bird? Am I more focused on my own selfish pursuits and the praise of others than on God's perfect plan for my life?*

I closed my eyes and released my thoughts to drift.

Unbidden, my mind filled with the image of a woman in dim light, a solitary figure on her knees. She appeared to be cast in nearly the same position as the eagle bowing low within its confining crown. The woman's blond hair fell in a soft curtain around her lowered face. I had trouble making out the details. Something about the woman seemed out of focus.

I looked closer, trying to clarify what I was seeing. As I did, the woman appeared to change subtly. Her hair color was slowly *shifting*. As the seconds passed, it seemed to alternate between blond and gray, then gray and red, then auburn, brunette, and black. Everything about her seemed to be softly phasing, as if I were watching her through a gently turning kaleidoscope. At different moments she looked like an acquaintance at church, then a previous neighbor, then an old friend in high school.

Gradually something else became apparent. The kneeling woman was not alone.

Surrounding her was a "presence," slithering shapes hidden in shadow. These evil apparitions whispered in the darkness: "I hate it when she bows before *Him*. She does this from time to time when she hears something that moves her." "It's momentary pangs of guilt that drive her here, but she loves *us* too much to let go." "She's already so numb, so dead within her selfish ambitions, it takes few of us to control her now." "As long as she focuses on herself, she's nearly useless to the One." "It doesn't matter if she knows the words of the Book, as long as they stay in her head and not her heart, as long as she doesn't *live* them."

Only then did I realize the woman was not simply kneeling; she was *praying*.

Still cast in a position of supplication, the woman held an object in each hand. Clutched with a white-knuckled grasp in her left was a spectacular bejeweled crown. It was obvious that it once fit perfectly on her head, for upon her brow was a deep, red groove. She'd worn the glorious, heavy decoration for a long while, perhaps even a lifetime. Firmly gripped in her right hand was a long, silver, extremely sharp, two-edged sword.

I watched the woman intently. Suddenly her entire body shuddered. She drew in a deep breath, opened her eyes, and slowly raised her head.

Methodically the woman rose so that she was balanced on one knee and one foot. Then she raised her arms, both items still locked in her grasp. Holding them out, she studied them, looking back and forth between the glamorous crown and the ordinary sword. One article was a magnificent adornment to be worn. The other was a common instrument designed, when wielded properly, to protect and serve. One garnered praise; the other gave assistance. One created envy; the other created freedom. One was designed to attract prideful attention and exalt its owner. The other was forged to defend the weak and exalt a King.

The woman continued to stare first at one object, then the other. Clearly, she was trying to make a choice between the two.

Then the woman's eyebrows came together. With intention she rose to her feet and balanced her weight. She raised the crown and the sword to eye level.

This was it... She was about to choose!

———————————— ⊰◈⊱ ————————————

9

THE BOULDER

Faithful Yesterday, Today, and Forever

"It's Sue's birthday! Let's climb South Sister to celebrate the birth of my dear friend!"

Since 1995 that annual milestone has been the only excuse I need to climb this fun peak on or near every June 23. South Sister is the largest of the Three Sisters mountains. These dramatic and beautiful volcanoes were originally named Faith, Hope, and Charity. At 10,358 feet Charity, South Sister, stands as Oregon's third largest peak, with an eleven-mile-round-trip trail that rises five thousand vertical feet to its broad summit. It's a straightforward hike that takes climbers to one of the best viewpoints in the state.

Because I can get inexperienced hikers to South Sister's glaciated summit, I love to take my staff and volunteers who come from abroad to see this incredible slice of the Northwest. Though Sue was out of town, a recent June morning presented the perfect opportunity—the weather was clear and cooperating. It looked to be an extraordinary day.

With ten of my ranch family in tow, I set off at the trailhead through a quiet hemlock forest. On our way up we passed a square boulder the size of my living room that had avalanched down a dozen years earlier. Since I used to train on this trail many times a week, I'd missed its fall by a *single* day. While tumbling for a quarter of a mile and carving a trench big enough for my truck to drive through, the behemoth snapped off enormous trees and scattered them like a child tossing a handful of pick-upsticks. Finally the boulder came to rest in the middle of the hiking trail. Never have I stood at its immense base and not admired the path of destruction that its descent left behind.

This gigantic boulder used to be part of a stone fortress towering over the roof of the forest. The life it once knew was that of a pillar within a colossal ridge high above. It was a boulder for the ages, or so thought every generation that once stood upon its broad shoulders. Now it sits on the lowly forest floor, dethroned of its former moorings of grandeur. Since it rests defiantly in the middle of the trail, the new path obediently detours around it.

After hiking about two miles, our group popped out of the deep forest and onto the Moraine Plains. Here the earth transformed from soft duff beneath towering boughs into dry, gray pumice. As the trees dropped behind us, we were greeted by massive vistas of South Sister, Broken Top, and Mount Bachelor.

Step by purposeful step, we moved closer toward our goal and ever-expanding views. It seemed impossible that the panorama could get any wider or better, yet the proof that filled our eyes with every mounting stride clearly proclaimed that it could. I've never climbed a mountain without pondering how closely it must resemble our walk with our King. Although each step takes effort, each one also makes us stronger. Strung together, those steps bring us closer to Him and into a beauty far beyond anything we've ever known or could even imagine.

About a mile from the summit, we carefully ascended the talus-strewn terminal moraine of Lewis Glacier. The reward of cresting its rim was to feast our eyes on the entire glacier sloping down into one of the most surreal green melt pools I've ever seen. Here we honored tradition by stopping to take in refreshments along with some indescribable views.

Recharged from the brief rest, we pressed on to the final summit push. Even the one-step-up, two-steps-back effect of hiking on loose scree couldn't dampen the thrill we felt from being in such a wondrous place.

By climbing the western ridge that flanks Lewis Glacier, we could look right into the yawning mouths of many deep blue crevasses.

Once we reached the summit crest, we strode across the broad crown toward the northeast ridge, where the true summit juts into view. Depending on the season, an ice blue teardrop pool often forms beneath the western ridge inside this nearly perfect volcanic cone. On this day all that was visible was a bright aqua depression where the water triumphantly bled through the icy snow, well on its way to becoming an ice-free pool.

Having scaled the last few hundred feet to the top, we rewarded ourselves by stopping at a suitable boulder near the edge to enjoy lunch with a view. Although I can't remember how the practice officially started, for some important reason every mountain that we climb in June has to be accompanied by a maturity-building cherry-pit-spitting contest off the summit.

I knew that this year my position as Exalted Queen of the Pits would be challenged by two young men who were eager to put my superhuman pit-spitting ability to the test. Once lunch was finished, Jeff, Sam, and I lined up near the edge of a precipice like pigeons on a wire. Each of us picked a boulder to perch on. I selected a trusted old friend of a rock that I've chosen to sit on—sometimes several times a year—since 1985.

Our preferred seating was ideal because of the abrupt downslope on the northern rim of the mountain. Beyond this slope, rock dropped almost vertically for nearly thirty feet, separating us from the upper reaches of the perilously steep Prouty Glacier. It was the perfect location for our pit-spitting challenge to begin. We passed around the bag of deep purple Bing cherry ammunition and steeled ourselves for the ensuing competition.

Sam's first attempt was pitiful. Jeff and I ended up wearing most of his effort, while his pit didn't even make a showing. In the best teeth-clenched, Clint Eastwood–ish smack talk I could muster, I said, "You spit like a little girl."

Even before Jeff's attempt I knew that my queen days might be numbered. He had the focus, intensity, and technique. He was trouble, all right! His first launch had distance but, thankfully, no arc. My superhero status was safe for the time being.

Unfortunately for me, with each shot the boys fired, they simply grew better and better. Soon I was pulling out all the stops by gripping my boulder on either side of my thighs, leaning back, and adding an extra whiplash with my upper body to get all the precious distance I could. Even so, Sam was gaining ground. Among his haphazard misfires, he sent a few that were truly home-run material. Meanwhile, Jeff, my blue-eyed opponent, continued to laugh sweetly in my face while handing me the pit-spitting spanking of a lifetime.

I still had a card to play, however. I was banking on the proven adage that "age and treachery will always triumph over youth and skill." For the benefit of my opponents, I paused dramatically, appearing to savor the delightful cherry pulp in my mouth. The reality behind my cherry-luvin' behavior was to conceal that I was analyzing the loose strands of my hair dancing in the breeze like a high-altitude, pit-spitting-duel-to-the-death windsock. The moment my hair fell straight was the same moment I knew there was clear air space to fire away.

My dastardly inspiration worked right up until…the earth moved—literally!

Without warning, the boulder I'd been sitting on with my legs dangling over its edge suddenly shifted. Even if I'd been equipped with springs attached to my backside, I wouldn't have moved away any faster. I'm not sure how I did it, but I sprang straight up and came down in a different area from where I started, probably looking much like a big, goofy jack-in-the-box. Jeff and Sam stared at me with the kind of open-mouthed wonder they might express if they were watching the space shuttle lift off.

At this point any explanation probably would have bounced off their already sky-high eyebrows. All I could do was point at my boulder and say, "It moved! My rock moved!"

I scooched forward and tapped the large stone a few times with the heel of my boot. The entire boulder suddenly split in half and began crumbling in on itself. What was left of the rock I'd been perched on, the very one I'd sat on for nearly two decades of trips to this mountain, disappeared over the edge in a crushing, chaotic fall.

I swung my legs behind me and leaned over and watched my old friend tumble and spin through the air. It fractured into more irreparable pieces with every impact against the rock wall. Reduced to little more than a hail of heavy gravel, the once great boulder disappeared forever into the glacier below.

Jeff, Sam, and I raised our chins and wordlessly looked at one another. I watched my boys silently move off their boulders, farther away from the edge. What appeared to be permanent wasn't. Just like my once-famed pit-spitting ability, my trusty old rock was no more.

FOREVER FAITHFUL

> Only God is worthy of our trust. Our King
> is forever faithful and unchanging.

No matter how stable things in this life might seem, nothing in this world is going to last—*nothing.*

I'd been sitting on the same giant boulder for years. I felt sure it couldn't fall. It was huge; it was immovable; it was part of a mountaintop! Yet right before my eyes, it broke into pieces and vanished.

In this life there is no amount of beauty or popularity, no amount of power and wealth, no amount of anything this world can supply that will keep us from crumbling or prevent us from dying.

The foundations of who we are and hope to become are formed in the deepest caverns of our souls, yet devastating fissures can reach even this sacred place. *Everything* is subject to this world's crushing, cracking forces of total destruction. When we choose to base our peace, our hope, our love, our salvation on temporary things, it stands to reason that these things are going to be temporary! At some point they *are* going to crumble and fall.

But when we put our peace, hope, love, and salvation in Jesus Christ alone, it's like putting them into a backpack and slinging them into heaven. They're *eternally* safe. *Nothing* in this world can touch them. There is no feeling, no event, no disease, no confrontation, no collapse or catastrophe this life can deal out that can steal what Jesus Christ gave His life to secure for us.

At some point we will all experience our best-laid plans being obliterated in a single moment. An accident, a disease, an addiction, an infidelity, a discovery, a choice—each can exact life-changing consequences. These catastrophic events not only have the potential to ruin us physically, but often and even more damaging, they also can destroy us emotionally. If we're not prepared, they can damage our faith as well.

At times I've been fickle with my passion and devotion. If we're honest with ourselves, we've all had seasons when we valued other things or people more than our Lord. Yet God is true. His love does not diminish when we reject Him. He is faithful forever.

Even when I chose to worship an eating disorder over my eternal King, He never abandoned me. He never shifted, cracked, or moved. His love for me remained just as strong as it had been from the beginning of time. My unfaithfulness to Him did not change, hinder, or diminish His faithfulness to me. He has been and always will be the only immovable truth we will ever know.

Sitting on that boulder up on South Sister, I felt completely assured. If anyone had questioned my safety, I would have answered, "I've sat on ledges my whole life. Oh, it's safe, all right. It's solid rock; it's secure. I've sat here for years. It was here before me and will be here after me."

Yet everything in this life is like that rock. The things we value might seem stable, secure, and immovable. A friendship, a marriage, a business deal, a church, a family, a home, a bank account, a reputation can all feel unshakable. Yet they're all subject to the world's freeze-and-thaw effects.

All things change but our God: "The LORD is my rock, my fortress, and my savior; my God is my rock, in whom I find protection. He is my shield, the strength of my salvation, and my stronghold, my high tower, my savior, the one who saves me from violence" (2 Samuel 22:2–3). "O LORD God Almighty! Where is there anyone as mighty as you, LORD? *Faithfulness is your very character*" (Psalm 89:8).

Friend, our only hope is Jesus Christ.

He is the same "yesterday, today, and forever" (Hebrews 13:8). He is the *only* constant we will ever know. He doesn't shift, He doesn't change, He never crumbles, and He never, *ever* falls.

10

THE CAGE

All-Consuming Peace

I wanted to see them face to face, to look into their eyes without fear.

My husband and I, along with nine other passengers in swim gear, rose and fell with the large swells that rolled under our boat. The wind whipped the surface of the Pacific Ocean into peaks of white foam. Waves smashed against our small vessel as we cautiously approached orange buoys that lined the top of the cage floating in the water. With boat, buoys, and cage heaving out of sync, the captain carefully aligned each and quickly lashed everything together.

This man and his seemingly casual manner intrigued me. He was topped with a turbulent crown of wavy red hair. His quick smile was framed by a constellation of freckles that did not stay confined to his cheeks. He was adorned with many tattoos, one of which I recognized as a tuna. Written upon his skin was the tale of a fisherman at heart.

With a wry smile the captain turned and asked, "Who wants to be first?" Troy and I glanced at the others in the boat. They instantly looked down at their feet. My eyes found Troy's and read his thoughts, which mirrored my own: *This is what we're here for. Let's go!* Together we went over the railing and into the cage with all the speed and poise of two clay pigeons at a trapshooting contest. The captain might as well have shouted, "Pull!"

Though the cage looked to be six feet square and about seven feet deep, I was glad that Troy and I were the only two inside it. Because both of us are large, diving to the bottom for the best viewing was going to be a trick. We apologized in advance for the certainty that we were about to repeatedly kick each other in the head.

Bobbing like a top in the dark, cobalt waters, I fitted my mask and snorkel to my face and gave the crew on the deck a thumbs-up. The cage that held Troy and me was released from the proximal safety of the small boat to float in exotic seas that were several hundred feet deep.

Quickly we drifted away. It wasn't long before I noticed how big the horizontal spaces were in the cage that surrounded us. The steel bars looked to be about nine inches wide on the sides and nearly twelve inches apart on the floor. Even my big feet had plenty of room to inadvertently slip through. Just the idea of this made my long toes curl into white fists. Without conscious thought my knees slowly rose to draw my feet as close to my torso as flexibility would allow. The upper half of the cage was made of Plexiglas, so it appeared as though nothing separated me from the great deep.

Trying to peer in all directions at once, I was never more aware of the vastness of the sea. Even though the weather was tempestuous, the ocean's color gradation was not. It was completely pristine. Few times have I seen such a perfect gradation, from the lightest blue all the way to the darkest indigo imaginable.

Because my view bled out equally in all directions into the blue expanse, it felt as if I were in the center of a massive void. Perhaps this is what it would be like to be awake while dreaming. Despite the fact that I'd been tossed about on the surface, once I dove under the waves, each way I turned my mask, I was rewarded with exactly the same flawless, undisturbed panorama.

Like soldiers covering each other, Troy and I bounced around back to back. I tickled his shoulder, and he turned to look at my face. I was amused by what I saw. My 230-pound, six-foot-three-inch man had reduced himself to a sphere roughly the size of a basketball! He was probably thinking the same thing I was. Taking his hand in mine, I squeezed it in anticipation. He squeezed back and squinted—an expression I recognized as a don't-flood-your-mask smile.

While bobbing in the cage, I took deep breaths to fill my lungs. Doing so made me more buoyant; I could float like a cork without touching the steel slats that confined me. Looking straight down, I strained to catch any movement, any interruption within the seamless, vast depths beneath me.

Then, like a phantom, a large shadow began to materialize. The dark apparition rose out of the black void below. This was what we'd been waiting for—a shark.

Gliding with unseen wings, the sea predator traversed its environment with fluid grace. As if homing in on a beacon, it purposefully moved toward us. I saw that it was a Galápagos shark, easily distinguished by its large, sickle-shaped tail. It looked to be around eight feet in length.

Swimming in slow arcs, each smaller than the last, the shark circled us like a tetherball winding around a pole. With each pass I could see more beautiful details of this amazing creature.

At first glance the shark appeared gray. But as it swam closer to look at us, we were able to look more closely at it. While dark gray clothed the upper half of the shark's body, below the snout crest it was nearly white. The tips of its pectoral fins and tail were tinged with a dusky wash that darkened into pure black. Its eyes were small and unblinking. With yellowish gray lenses surrounding vertical pupils, the shark's eyes had a demonish quality.

Now, as it glided only a few feet away, I saw detailed rows of serrated teeth lining the familiar open-mouthed grimace. The fact that this shark was so large only added to the impact of the moment.

With the lightness of a butterfly, it ran the rim of its snout along the Plexiglas that separated us. I could literally see into its mouth. Like a prisoner placing her palm on the glass that separates her from a visitor, I put my flat hand over the area the shark touched. Though my hand appeared to be only three inches from its eye, the gray creature never flinched. It only continued to circle inquisitively while staring at me with its unblinking gaze.

Troy rammed me hard from behind with his elbow. I quickly turned and saw that we were not alone. Other sharks were rapidly closing in on nearly every side. Having been so entranced by the one, I didn't see the others until they were nearly touching our enclosure.

Close to a dozen sharks circled. They darted toward and around the cage in a mesmerizing dance. Wanting a closer look, I took a deep breath and dove to the bottom of the cage. While carefully holding on to the floor slats, I was better able to observe their movements below us. Again and again I dove to the bottom of the cage. I didn't want to miss a moment of this amazing scene.

Suddenly the attitude of the sharks changed. They seemed to stiffen. In the same instant a prickle ran up my neck. I caught movement out of the corner of my eye and turned. The new arrival was only inches from me and utterly enormous!

This marauder of the deep was several feet longer than any of the other suitors, with an equally impressive girth. I knew she had to be a female because of her bulk. She appeared slightly lighter gray than the others, perhaps because she was just so huge. I watched her propel herself with strong, graceful strokes of her crescent tail. The newly arrived shark's massive size and direct movements commanded the other sharks to retreat. And they did.

Drawn by intense curiosity, this gargantuan beast soared around us several times before casually testing our Plexiglas enclosure with intentional bumps of her long, rounded snout. The shark's gaping mouth framed with spiny teeth was the very picture of pure annihilation for anything that ventured out of our protective shelter.

I could hear the voice of our captain echoing in my ears: "Don't put anything outside the cage that you want to keep! These sharks are coming to look for a meal. They're intending to feed themselves. Don't reach out of the cage, or you could become part of their breakfast!"

I watched the giant shark glide around me and doubted I'd ever been more aware or more appreciative of a safe place to abide in. Believe me when I say there was nowhere in the water I'd have rather been at that moment. Without instruction, debate, or convincing, this space was where I wanted to reside. Of *course* I was going to stay in the cage!

I tried to imagine what I would feel like if I were somehow suddenly washed out of our protective position. The pitch and roll of our enclosure was violent at times. More than once I was slammed against the bars. Would I still be so euphoric and unafraid if I was outside this zone of security?

Even while dangling like bait in a box, I felt only absolute awe, because I trusted the glass and metal cage around me. I could hardly believe I was actually getting to do this! I was in the Pacific, I was safe, and I was surrounded by an entire league of gigantic, saw-toothed predators.

Slowly I realized that it didn't matter what swam around me or how ferocious they were or even how many there were. As long as I abided in this safe place, I could swim through anything.

I should have been terrified, but I wasn't. I was completely at peace.

A Place of Peace

Truly, our King is peaceful.

God is so good to reveal Himself, whether it's through His Word, in church, or with a shark cage in the Pacific Ocean. When we're *in* Christ, it's as if we're inside the invisible safety of a Plexiglas box. We can swim among giant "sharks" and have complete peace. When we're *not* in Christ, we're not in a safe place. Then swimming among giant sharks is terrifying because one of them could destroy us at any moment.

Since we know this, why do we believers keep climbing out of Christ's protective place?

Friend, when we're in Christ, we will have perfect peace…no matter what monsters, what storms, what darkness surrounds us. He cannot be moved, and when we place our lives inside His, *neither can we.*

His peace is not circumstantial. It doesn't come from those things on the outside that surround us. His peace comes from within; it comes from Jesus being inside us. Scripture says, "His peace will guard your hearts and minds as you live *in* Christ Jesus" (Philippians 4:7). If we're finding our peace in Christ, nothing in this life can take it away—period!

Since this is true, why do we Christians suffer from bouts of anxiety, depression, and fear? Why are such vast numbers mired in negativity? Maybe it's because our focus really isn't "in" Christ. Perhaps we've placed our trust and hopes for peace in a husband, a job, a friend, a look, an ability, a bank account, a family member, a title, a boyfriend, a thing. Any of these entities, when placed in a higher position than God, becomes more than just a distraction from truth; it becomes our *idol.* When it wavers or collapses, so does the sense of peace we fostered through it.

When will we realize that where fear exists, peace cannot?

Someone much wiser than I once said, "Either Christ is Lord *of* all… or He isn't Lord *at* all."

When we continually jump in and out of the peace of God, it's the equivalent of playing spiritual Hokey Pokey. He doesn't want us to put our trust in Him and then take our trust out. Or put our trust in Him and shake it all about. Believe me, this *isn't* what it's all about! He'd rather we just put our hearts in…and keep them in, because it's when we *abide in* Him that His authentic peace within us grows.

Resting in God's peace is like being in a shark cage or the eye of a hurricane. It doesn't mean we will be spared from those who wish to harm us or from the storms of this life. It means that because of our King's great love for us, we can go *through* the storms together, in peace: "I am leaving you with a gift—peace of mind and heart" (John 14:27). Because of our Lord, we *can* be peaceful in the face of serious illness or injury, we *can* be peaceful in the collapse of a family, we *can* be peaceful in financial crisis, and we *can* be peaceful when facing death—if we choose to place our peace in Him.

So if we don't feel God's peace, it's only because we've chosen not to. Inadvertently or not, we've left the Plexiglas box and are swimming with creatures that can destroy us. If this is true for you, there's no time like the present to call on His name and return to His presence and peace.

David once sang, "But when I am afraid, I put my trust in you. O God, I praise your word. I trust in God, so why should I be afraid? What can mere mortals do to me?" (Psalm 56:3–4). Because our eternal life is secure, we can relax in any circumstance. We already know that—no matter what—we will soon be with Christ *forever.* This life isn't our end, and this world isn't our home. We're living in a tryout, a practice run for eternity with our King.

The simple truth is this: when we really *know* who God is, we will fear *nothing.* Because "nothing can ever separate us from his love. Death can't, and life can't. The angels can't, and the demons can't. Our fears for today, our worries about tomorrow, and even the powers of hell can't keep God's love away" (Romans 8:38). Since our lives are in God's hands, we're immune to death until we arrive at His appointed time.

My friend, even in the worst-case scenarios known to humankind, God is right beside us. He is our shield. He is our shark cage. He is our shelter in the stormy times. He is the light that pierces any darkness, "and the darkness can never extinguish it" (John 1:5). He has *already* overcome every fear we will ever face.

This world defines peace as the absence of conflict, but God's peace is confident assurance in *any* circumstance.

Real peace doesn't come when God takes our problems away. It comes when we firmly, deeply, genuinely put our faith in Him.

It's time for us to stop choosing to live in fear.

Be encouraged. His peace is a box, a space that no fear can penetrate: "I prayed to the LORD, and he answered me, freeing me from *all* my fears.

Those who look to him for help will be radiant with joy; no shadow of shame will darken their faces. I cried out to the LORD in my suffering, and he heard me. He set me free from all my fears. For the angel of the LORD guards all who fear him, and he rescues them. Taste and see that the LORD is good. Oh, the joys of those who trust in him!" (Psalm 34:4–8).

Because of our Lord's great love for us, He has prepared a place where we can come out of the storms, heartache, and hardship of this world and into His all-consuming peace. It is not found in a box or in a cage. It is found only in His very presence, which knows no boundary at all.

11

THE GIFT

Extraordinary Favor

Often my life feels like a treasure chest. Hardly a day goes by that I don't reflect on the incredible gifts I've been so honored to receive. My home is filled with cards, photographs, drawings, hand lotions, quilts, treats, jewelry, and outdoor gear—all evidence of the kindness and good wishes of others.

Their generosity and imagination seem boundless. Occasionally I receive items that appear to have been the resourceful combination of what could be found under the backseat of the family vehicle. These crusty creations usually consist of leftover Happy Meal parts, petrified french fries, and other unknown mummified objects all ingeniously held together with wads of chewed gum. They're amazing! The sheer inspiration behind such gifts makes me crack up with laughter.

Upon one such presentation I caught the horrified stare of a visiting adult. Her expression declared, "I wouldn't be caught dead touching that rotten thing!" I'm grateful I don't feel the same way. It won't surprise me a bit if one of these days I'm found passed out on my ranch, wearing a big dumb grin on my face while clutching something really gross.

A gift is *a gift,* and it doesn't matter whether it's a crushed bunch of flowers yanked from my own garden, a half-eaten cookie, or color-smeared little hands dropping M&M'S directly into my mouth. The presents I receive are always a reminder of how much I'm loved.

No matter the gift, the old adage still rings true: it really *is* the thought that counts.

With this fact in mind, I knew the upcoming day would be incredible. Not because it was August or even because the weather was beautiful. It was the perfect day because it was my birthday.

Most people didn't know it was my birthday, which I like since folks then don't feel obligated to give me anything other than a genuine hug. I love a warm embrace. My grandmother taught me that no matter how hard times get, it's something everyone can afford to give.

Throughout the day as I was showered with cards, simple gifts, and a full bottle of water poured down my back, I knew that something else, something extraordinary, was on the way. It wasn't intuition. My friend Cheree had called to tell me her daughter, Jenna, had done something remarkable for my birthday. Cheree was so thrilled about the gift that she called to tell me how excited I soon would be.

Every time I thought of Cheree's call and the pure delight in her voice, I nearly felt like crying. Cheree was a single mother who had done her best to raise her daughter. This family of two worked remarkably hard simply to cover the basic necessities, things others don't give a second thought to. In years past this mother and daughter had used finances allotted for Christmas gifts to pay the mortgage. Their gift to each other was the opportunity to continue living in their modest home.

Each did her best to make ends meet. Cheree was employed by an insurance company, and Jenna balanced finishing her senior year of high school with working at our ranch. Despite all the challenges mother and daughter faced, their faith remained firm in Christ. Their finances were skinny, yet He'd never let them down. I was moved by their tenacity to keep pushing forward no matter what the world told them they couldn't do. Quite simply, they just *did*.

For me, being able to call them my friends was plenty gift enough.

It wasn't until the celebration of another ranch day was coming to a close that Jenna sought me out. Her faded jeans were a canvas of the work and fun she'd combined throughout the afternoon. Dirty circles on her knees told a tale of pulling weeds, while multicolored spatters of paint on her legs revealed she'd helped a little "artist" who'd delighted in making her horse a rainbow Appaloosa. Water marks from a recent run through the sprinklers completed Jenna's ranch fashion.

Together Jenna and I walked up the grassy hillside that leads to my home. She carried a beautifully wrapped box of substantial weight. Contemplating what could be so special and so heavy launched my curiosity into overdrive.

I held the front door open for Jenna as she led the way into my sunny kitchen. Standing between one wall that resembles a deep desert sunset and another colored to look like old parchment, she laid the package on the counter and indicated that I should open it. With a slight lift of her shoulders, my quiet girl said in a small voice, "It's something I've been working on for a while." The smile that followed was a sweet mix of shy and radiant excitement.

Jenna's clear blue eyes danced with anticipation as I began to unwrap her gift. Pure, innocent expectation filled the room like a rushing mountain stream. Whatever this item was, I knew that it meant a great deal to Jenna and that she loved it as well. The deeper I delved into the package, the more I felt her enthusiasm swell. My little kitchen was awash in a sloshing wave of eagerness that I would cherish her gift as much as she did.

Fully aware of her intent gaze on my face, I understood how enormously important the following moments would be. Whatever was about to happen clearly meant far more to her than simply giving me a birthday present. I knew this would be a very special moment between us.

Once the wrapping paper was off, I cut the heavy tape that held the package closed. I opened the box and was greeted with carefully placed crumpled wads of newspaper. This gift was heavy and breakable. Lifting out the last remaining layer of newsprint, I finally saw it. Recognition shot through my heart like an electric current! My voice collapsed beneath a tide of emotion.

I couldn't *believe* what I was seeing! I couldn't *believe* that Jenna was able to part with this beloved treasure! I couldn't *believe* that she was giving this honored prize *to me*!

Instantly I was transported to a scene that had occurred two months earlier. Together Jenna and I strode down the halls of her high school. She had invited me to attend an art show hosted there. This special night was marked by the awards ceremony. Her entry had won its category; soon she would be stepping up in front of a packed house to receive her award. Jenna also planned on giving a small presentation about Crystal Peaks and receiving a donation for the ranch from the school's art department.

As we walked shoulder to shoulder, I was pleasantly aware of just how beautiful she looked. Dressed in a simple light skirt, sleeveless top, and sandals, this tall, thin girl looked more elegant and striking than nearly any girl I'd ever seen. She was happy. Interestingly enough, it was her joy that transformed her. She was far beyond beautiful. She was radiant.

We entered the art department, where the show was being held. I walked behind Jenna as we carefully wove a serpentine path through the milling crush of students, parents, and art lovers. Once we reached the back wall, Jenna asked me to look through the pottery section.

It wasn't long before my attention was drawn to a lovely collection of wheel-thrown plates and bowls. What initially caught my eye was the color. Half the entry was a vibrant hue that looked like adobe, the other half a cobalt blue. Each piece was embedded with the same hand-stamped Aztecish pattern. Because the stamp was pressed into the surface of each item, the glaze pooled within the design, making it slightly darker than the rest of the piece. The effect of the artistic arrangement of the plates and bowls was absolutely charming. I noticed a handmade tag that identified the collective masterpiece as Jenna's.

"You made these?" I inquired and declared at the same time. Jenna was standing slightly behind me when I turned to look into her face. Sunlight bouncing off water would've paled in comparison to her smile. It didn't really matter that her entry had won. What she'd made was beautiful. She knew it was special. She knew that what was displayed before us was her absolute best. This young woman, who possessed so little by worldly standards, had created something truly extraordinary.

Now, inside my kitchen, lovingly cushioned by secondhand newspapers in an old cardboard box, were Jenna's beautiful plates and bowls.

To some, her gift might not have had any greater value than a widow's mite. But to me it was absolutely priceless. I don't remember the words that passed between us during the moments of freeing her gift from its newspaper cocoon. Whatever they might've been, I know they were paltry compared to the weight of emotion I felt. I knew what this gift meant to Jenna, and I knew what it cost her to give it up.

Even though this was the very best and most beloved thing she'd ever created, she willingly gave it all—to *me*.

Now I was the new keeper of the gift.

After that, whenever I entertained company or the ranch staff came up to the house for dinner, I used Jenna's lovely plates to serve snacks. Her largest bowl was set in a place of prominence in my kitchen so its decorative grace could bless everyone who entered. And since I was the one who entered most often, I was the one who was most blessed. Hardly a day went by when I wasn't deeply moved—again—by the significance of this remarkable gift.

I couldn't have known it then, but the impact of Jenna's gift was about to increase beyond anything I could have imagined.

Several months after I received the gift, my phone rang late one night. The news was horrific. There was a fire.

Though firefighters did all they could, the simple home that Cheree and Jenna shared was completely destroyed by flames. A faulty strand of Christmas lights was to blame. Thankfully, Cheree and Jenna were not home when the fire broke out, so neither was harmed. The same could not be said for the small manufactured home they had worked so hard to maintain. The inferno destroyed everything. Jenna shared how hard it was to sift through the charred remains of all they loved: "You don't even realize how much you've lost until you find a fragment of a childhood toy, a scrap of a cherished photograph, or the blackened remains of prize ribbons you won on your very first horse."

What the flames didn't directly take, the intense heat and dense smoke did. Nothing in their home survived.

That is, almost nothing. In the months that followed, out of the ash something beautiful began to emerge.

Family, friends, and neighbors came together to help in a myriad of wonderful ways. With some assistance from their insurance company and the combined efforts of many, before long a brand-new home was up, and Cheree and Jenna were moving in.

It was immediately after their housewarming that I realized I'd brought the wrong gift. Their new home had some lovely items inside but didn't feel like *their* home. It wasn't until I was lying in bed that night, contemplating the day, that I realized why it seemed so different. Though their new house was adorned with nice things, none of them carried sentimental value. None were *their* things.

So I showed up on their new doorstep with another gift for their home. With a Cheshire cat grin, I was now the one bringing the old cardboard box into their bright new kitchen.

I set the box on a bar that separated the kitchen from the dining area. Before I even opened the box, Cheree started to cry... She already knew what rare treasure lay inside. Jenna hugged me tight and simply whispered, "Thank you." As if waiting for the gift's homecoming, an empty wooden display area lay vacant, ready to be filled.

Jenna's extraordinary plates and bowls had finally come home.

Giving and Keeping Our Best

Our King is the Author of hope.

Shortly after returning Jenna's cherished dishes to her care, I was again lying in bed at night, reflecting on the day. It was during this quiet time that the voice of my King began to speak: *Child, you were able to give back to Jenna what she gave you. Had she given you nothing, that is exactly what you would have been able to return. It was with great love that she chose not to give you her leftovers or excess. Instead, she chose to give you her very best. It was precisely because of her selflessness that you were able to keep her treasure safe from the fire and then give it back to her when she needed it most— when the timing was perfect.*

My girl, this is exactly what I wish for you to do with Me.

Will you trust Me with your very best? A fire is coming at the end of your days that nothing in this life can withstand…except what you select to willingly give Me. Understand that the things you choose to entrust to Me, you will have forever. But the things that you choose to hold on to will all perish.

I am hope. I never change; I never waver or fade. I abide far beyond any thief, fire, or economic boundary. Life is but a breath, and everything this world toils and clamors to gain will perish with its possessor. The only things that will endure the coming inferno will be the things you release to Me. Unlike the impostors of this world, I will keep whatever you place in My care far beyond any decay, destruction, or demolition. If you firmly choose to place your soul in Me, nothing in this world—not even death—can steal it away. I will hold you close for all eternity.

As I've considered those holy words since that night, I've often asked, *Lord, am I giving You my excess, or am I giving You my very best? On that day when I will stand before You, are You going to give me a crown the size of a Cheerio because all I ever gave You was my junk? Or are You going to return something extraordinary…because that's what I did my very best to entrust to You?*

When we place our hope in Christ, it's like putting everything we value—our hope, love, joy, peace, faith, and forgiveness—in a box and giving it to Christ. Once He has our hope, it's secure—*eternally* secure. The enemy cannot steal, destroy, or even touch it. There's nothing in, on, under, or above this world that can change the security of our hope. Once I have chosen to entrust Christ with my hope, the only one who can change its status is *me*.

I'm the only one who can choose to take my hope out of Christ and place it in other things—my appearance, boyfriend, new job, relationship, marriage, education, friendships, family, bank account. All these things are subject to change. All these things will eventually perish.

Our nonbelieving society calls the masses to live in a dream world of wealth, beauty, power, and acceptance. However, a dream world exists only in the mind of the dreamer. It's our choice alone not to let our life's goals be so dreamy and unreal that we awaken too late and miss the reality of God's truth.

Real hope is no dream. It cannot be purchased with riches, popularity, or worldly security. Genuine hope comes from an honest, growing relationship with our Lord. It comes from our King alone.

Our King is the hope of all people and all nations: "You faithfully answer our prayers with awesome deeds, O God our savior. You are the hope of everyone on earth" (Psalm 65:5).

Our Lord is able to keep all that we have committed to Him and save it until the day we stand face to face with Him. We can trust ourselves to the God who made us because He will never fail us. Because of His promises to us, how can we not reach for the truth of Hebrews 10:23: "Without wavering, let us hold tightly to the hope we say we have, for God can be trusted to keep his promise"?

We serve a Lord who is the Author of creating and giving gifts. His own Word declares, "Whatever is good and perfect comes to us from God above" (James 1:17). He is never bankrupt. When we place our hope and our value in Him, we too will become rich in all the ways that matter most.

He isn't keeping plates and bowls… He's keeping *us*.

Editor's Note: Read more about Jenna and Cheree in the stories "Simple Gifts," found in Kim's book *Hope Rising,* and "Cleansing Fire," found in Kim's book *Bridge Called Hope.*

12

THE WILDERNESS

He Leads Us Home

Over three hundred. That's how many horses our team at Crystal Peaks Youth Ranch has helped save and introduce to a second chance at life. One of the four pillars of our organization is to "rescue the equine." I've been salvaging horses since 1995 and thought I'd seen it all. Sadly, I was wrong.

Troy and I were driving home through the desolate Oregon outback, traveling over a golden roller coaster of undulating hills. The late October afternoon was framed by low, cloudy, lavender skies, adding to the unique drama and beauty of the high desert. As we crested the top of another grassy knoll, I was startled by the ring of my cell phone. It was my dear friend Sue.

Our conversation had hardly started before my reception was cut off. Establishing connection was like trying to catch a rock skipping off the top of waves, as we had only a few seconds of reception on the high points of the road. Through her broken messages I was able to piece together that Sue was calling about a horse in need. He'd been found in the wilderness and was severely injured. Would we take him?

I was able to respond in the affirmative before our sporadic communication was lost completely. We would have to drive the remaining five hours home to hear the rest of the story.

Upon arriving at the ranch, Troy and I learned that our new sight-unseen horse was a small six-year-old gelding that had staggered into a hunters' camp during the night. The horse's wounds were so serious that the outdoorsmen called the U.S. Forest Service to send a ranger to hike in and euthanize him. The woman assigned this task evaluated him and saw he was still fighting for his life. Encouraged by his will to live, she led him down the mountainside under the brilliant light of a full moon and into a waiting horse trailer.

The region where the horse was located was high in the wilderness of the Cascade Range, yet his halter and dragging lead rope showed the dark bay Arab gelding was certainly not wild. Instead, the rescued horse was kind and gentle, quietly submitting to everyone who sought to care for him. While being led out of the wilderness and transported for emergency treatment, he behaved like a wounded gentleman. Those who assisted him estimated he'd been wandering for weeks. He looked to be about two hundred pounds underweight, an enormous amount for a small horse, and was incredibly dehydrated.

At the hospital it was confirmed—his wounds were severe.

I pulled my truck to a stop in front of the Bend Equine Medical Center. Rarely have I parked in their yard and not felt deeply grateful that the one equine surgery center serving the entire eastern half of our state is just three miles from my ranch. After working many difficult cases with them, I'd learned to trust this remarkable group of veterinarians and their assistants. This team's combined dedication and compassion move me to love them not merely as friends but more like family.

I had barely pushed through the hospital doors when I was besieged by a landslide of information. When the small horse was admitted and led into the trauma center, his condition was immediately assessed. Remnants of a green elasticized bandage had grown into the gelding's left front leg and effectively become a tourniquet. As the tattered bandage was carefully cut away, nearly all the flesh beneath it sloughed off as well. Adding further to the suffering of the abandoned bay was a horrific open gash on the back of his left front cannon. The infected wound had festered so much that its rotten stench filled the room. Once the layers of caked blood, pus, and biomatter were removed, the working tendons of his leg were clearly visible.

While my friends washed their new patient's leg, they noticed a heavy trail of crusted blood that traveled up his leg, shoulder, and neck. This hideous path provided further evidence of the severity of his injuries. Blood tests showed that the small gelding's plight was even more precarious than initially thought. Through the trauma of his injuries, he had lost fully *half* of his total blood volume—for a horse his size, nearly four gallons! In their combined careers the attending vets had never seen a horse lose so much blood—and live.

Next came the obvious question: where had the blood loss come from?

The team followed the dried-blood trail to the horse's left eye. It was completely destroyed and hanging out of the socket. So putrid was its bloody surface that much of his long black forelock had adhered to it and needed to be cut off. The damaged eye would have to be removed once his blood volume was restored to a normal level. Behind his horrifying eye, they found a small, ominous depression.

As bad as his eye injury was, his head injury was much worse.

The x-rays revealed the unthinkable. This gentle little horse with the kind spirit had been shot in the head...*twice.*

Looking at his x-rays, I was aghast at the meaning. Someone had shot this placid soul through his left eye with a solid bullet and then again, three inches behind his left eye, with a hollow point. The trajectory of the second bullet traveled through the top of his lower jaw, shattering it. The bullet continued to penetrate his skull as it exploded into dozens of jagged—and inoperable—fragments of shrapnel.

I looked at him for the first time and couldn't believe he'd endured so much.

The little Arabian had survived for weeks with a horrifically infected leg wound, a broken jaw, a destroyed eye, and lethal blood loss. He managed this feat with the remains of two bullets scattered throughout his head. If all this weren't bad enough, he was also left to wander in a high-altitude forest while dragging a lead rope. Any one of these afflictions could have easily killed him. Inexplicably, he'd survived them all.

Now, here he was standing before me in an intensive care room. From under a turban of bandages, he blinked inquisitively at me with his one remaining eye. It was a miracle he was standing at all! I noticed that his hind legs were splayed out in a weakened effort to maintain his feeble balance.

I shoved back the heavy door and quietly entered his white cement room. Though the gelding's head was bandaged, one leg was tightly wrapped from hoof to knee, and he had catheters embedded in both sides of his neck, he reached out to me. Despite his fragile state, he wanted to give me what he had, the gift of equine encouragement. Though the small gelding was so diminished from dehydration, malnutrition, and infection that he could hardly stand, he expended the extra effort to greet me. As I extended the palm of my hand to his offered muzzle, incredulous wonder filled my heart.

Unfortunately, this simple gesture was more than he could bear. While leaning toward me, he suddenly lost his balance and began to fall. In the process he knocked me against the cinder-block wall, and we fell to the floor together.

Thankfully, we were both unhurt by the tumble, and I was able to help roll him back up to his feet. With his head hung low and his hind legs looking like Bambi's on ice, his remaining eye expressed equine embarrassment—I assumed for knocking me to the floor. Even in his mortal state, his only concern appeared to be for me. After surviving the ultimate human betrayal, this little horse still had hope that there were good people in the world, and he dared to believe that I was one of them. Though he had no reason to, he still chose to forgive and trust.

What a spirit. What a horse. There in an equine intensive care room, I realized that I wanted to be more like him...because he was more like Jesus.

With both hands on his shoulder and my hip braced against the wall, I helped him find his balance again. "Oh, little man, we're all right," I whispered. "Everything is going to be all right."

I gently rubbed the bay's neck and back. In a voice only he could hear, I said, "You're going to be okay, sweet boy. You're safe now. All is well. You're going to get through this, you'll see. We'll do it together."

Once the bullets were discovered, a full investigation was launched. Clearly, this was not an accidental shooting committed by an overeager hunter. Neither did it look like the mercy killing of a mortally wounded or old, decrepit horse. The beautiful gelding was not even fully grown. His leg wound was terrible but certainly not fatal. This shooting was done at close range with two different types of ammunition.

The mystery surrounding the small horse grew when his caregivers and I noticed his feet. Not only were his hoofs well trimmed, but they also had fresh nail holes. This indicated he'd worn a full set of shoes that had only recently been removed. Something else that caught our attention was several white spots on the top of his abnormally high withers. Someone had ridden this horse with a saddle that fit so poorly it wore the skin right off his back, leaving behind several telltale white scars.

There was another compelling clue. Though the gelding was very thin, his coat exhibited health dapples, a condition that results from horses being exposed to excellent feed over time. In response to the nutrition, vague dappling will present throughout the coat and will usually cover the shoulders, sides, and rump.

Without words this little horse was telling us he had belonged to someone. He'd recently been a very healthy gelding wearing a full set of shoes and had been ridden enough with an ill-fitting saddle to have incurred sizable scars.

From all the evidence, the medical staff at Bend Equine and I deduced that someone felt this horse's leg wound was just too much to deal with. Somehow they believed that loading up their friend and driving him to a remote location to be destroyed was their best option.

Our working scenario was that the perpetrator had shot the gelding through the left eye with a solid bullet. Astonishingly, this did not kill him. Apparently this person then reloaded with a hollow-point round—designed to kill—and shot him again three inches behind the left eye. We believed the young horse fell to the ground, knocked unconscious from the impact. Thinking he was dead, the perpetrator left the scene. Bleeding profusely from his wound, the small horse then lost half of his blood volume.

Miraculously, the gelding awoke. Somehow summoning the strength to stand, he lurched to his feet and staggered away. He refused to give up. In the face of impossible odds, he continued to put one foot in front of the other, step after step, until he walked through his wilderness.

In the following weeks I spent time nearly every day with our new boy. I didn't wish another minute of this abandoned horse's life to pass without his knowing that he was cherished, that he belonged to someone and had a loving home waiting for him. I wanted this horse to understand he had a new family now that already loved him very much.

Surprisingly, even though his wounds were grave, his spirit was not.

Amid great pain and some necessary unpleasant care, he was still happy. Every day, once he heard my voice down the hall, he called out to me. Inside his intensive care ward, from beneath the pirate bandage that covered and supported his damaged eye, he would whinny a greeting. I always imagined him saying, "Hey, girl who loves me, I'm down heeeeeere!"

Immediately we became very dear, very close friends. Yet he proved that I was not his only friend; he adopted the entire staff at the hospital as well. His actions confirmed that he was an incredibly thankful little horse. He was grateful to have been rescued, to be receiving care even through pain, and to be loved.

To keep his spirits buoyed during his extensive healing process, I often drove truckloads of kids from the ranch to spend time with him. Though his head and eye were heavily wrapped and he was enduring great pain, he always took the time to acknowledge every child that came to give him a kiss and a hug. Soon the door of his hospital room was papered with cards, letters, and colorful, clumsy drawings made by those whose only wish was for him to get well so he could come home.

His strength slowly improved. When the weather allowed, the supportive staff at the hospital turned my new boy out into a small outdoor enclosure. It was here that I often brought a writing tablet and pen and just sat with my friend in the weak sun of late winter. Sometimes I brushed him, sometimes I scratched all his itchy places, and sometimes, when he seemed to be struggling with the pain, I softly sang to him.

When I finally sat down to write, he would often join me. He circled like a dog looking for just the right spot, then folded up his legs and gently lay down beside me. A few times I was honored to have him succumb to lying completely flat. Once he was stretched out, it was only a matter of moments before he serenaded me with the peaceful sound of complete equine trust—he snored.

During this season of recovery, I learned a great deal about my remarkable friend. He was courageous and happy. He was a survivor who'd fought hard to live, to keep going. Most horses would have perished when faced with just one of his symptoms. Yet he survived what many would consider insurmountable odds. The more I pondered our gelding, the more I realized just how symbolic he was of the vast majority *of us.*

At some point in life, nearly all of us go through horrible, unthinkable times. We feel as if we've been led into the wilderness, perhaps by those we loved and trusted, beaten badly, and left for dead. We stumble away, wandering within the desolation of loneliness, unable to help ourselves, unable to stop the hemorrhaging, unable to find our way home. Our horizon of hope begins to fade into gray. Death looms.

Yet so often in this place—our darkest night, our deepest wilderness, our greatest despair—when our hope is bleeding out, we call on His name, and *He comes.* Jesus Christ enters the wreckage of our hearts, our blackest place, our wasteland of hopelessness, and He leads us *home.*

Continued reflection about my sweet boy revealed something else. Like a soldier returning from battle or a small horse from the wilderness, we too can choose to fall into the welcome arms of those who love us. We, like the soldier or horse, might not look the same on the outside as we did when we left. When we come home from our battle in the wilderness, we might be scarred or disfigured. Yet according to one extremely wise, eight-year-old ranch volunteer, all of us have potential to be hero material—not because of how we look, but because of what we've done and can do. As he so eloquently stated about his wounded, four-legged friend, "It's not his outside that makes him so lovable. It's the *inside* that I love. It's not what the outside looks like that makes him a hero. It's the inside. It's his heart—that's what makes him a *real* hero."

Since my wounded horse was such an incredible symbol of redemption, mercy, and salvation, I decided to name him in honor of those who've chosen to serve our great country with their lives and those who've chosen to reach for the hand of the Lord and walk through their personal wilderness. His name became Hero.

After four months in intensive care, my little Hero was ready to come home to a true hero's welcome. The news about his undying hope had spread. While pulling up the ranch driveway with my sweet four-legged son in tow, I could hardly believe the sight that greeted us. Over three hundred people had gathered from all over the Northwest to usher this once-abandoned horse into his new life. I drove up the driveway through a cheering hallway of waving arms, all reaching out to embrace the little horse that wouldn't quit. The ranch was bursting with men, women, and children who'd come to invite this kind soul into his new family.

While slowly maneuvering through the applauding crowd, I was struck by a thought: *Is this what it feels like to finally enter heaven? Is this how our family members who've gone on before will receive us? Will they be cheering, embracing, crying, reaching for us in love and welcome? I hope so.*

Once the trailer door was opened, Hero stood looking out over the crowd with his one remaining eye. Instead of being terrified by all the commotion, the cheering and clapping, the only expression on his face was one of joy.

He'd shown everyone the truth in Psalm 23:4: "Even when I walk through the dark valley of death, I will not be afraid, for you are close beside me." He chose not to stay in his place of suffering but to walk *through* his "dark valley of death." Because he did, he encouraged others to do the same.

He'd made it. Hero was finally *home.*

Out of the Wilderness

Our King is loving and merciful, always ready
to lead us home.

Since Hero has come home, his amazing account has continued to roll like a healing wave across this nation. On the following Christmas Day, his miraculous story of survival was featured on the front page of the largest newspaper in Oregon. Amid the flood of well-wishing cards, e-mails, letters, and phone calls, one seemed to sum up what a great number expressed. It came in a legal-size envelope with no return address or identification. It contained only a small note, which read, "I was thinking of ending it all. Then I read about Hero—and changed my mind. Because he didn't give up, I won't. Thank you."

My little Hero is only a tiny reflection of my *real* hero: Jesus Christ.

It is Christ alone who is the true champion. He walked through the wasteland of death itself. Jesus is the only One who chose to come into my unique wilderness of sorrow. Out of love, He did it for me, and He has done it throughout history for every soul who ever turned to Him: "For God so loved the world that he gave his only Son, so that everyone who believes in him will not perish but have eternal life" (John 3:16).

Jesus is the only One who laid down His life as the bridge of hope by which we can escape our wasteland of pain and enter His joy.

The choice to cross that bridge is left to every soul. We can opt to stay in our wilderness and be frustrated, angry, negative, self-justified, and

sorrowful. Or we can reach out to the hand that has always reached for ours and cross the bridge of His mercy into His presence, His love, His redemption, and His freedom: "If you wander beyond the teaching of Christ, you will not have fellowship with God. But if you continue in the teaching of Christ, you will have fellowship with both the Father and the Son" (2 John verse 9).

At some point each of us will face tremendous heartache. It's especially during these times of wandering through the backwoods of despair that we must seek our Lord's mercy. His desire is that we give our burdens to Him. Yet inexplicably, we often try to carry them ourselves.

Why do we willingly step into and inhabit this place when the Lord has clearly marked a path by which we can escape? It's true; life can be hard, but our hearts don't have to be. Life can be burdensome and dark, but our attitudes don't have to be. Life can be sad, but because our joy is not founded in the things of this world, *we* don't have to be.

The first kid to ride Hero was a fifteen-year-old girl named Heather. "I've endured great suffering in my life," Heather says. "Many times I gave up trusting in people, and I nearly gave up trusting in God. At times I thought nobody cared or understood. But then Hero came along, and he *did* understand. Those he put his trust in betrayed him. He could've just lain down and died, something I've often longed to do. But he didn't. He kept going and going, and when he couldn't go any longer, God rescued him. I just want to cry when I think about my friendship with Hero. He reminds me of what Jesus did for me, and because of that, I talk to Jesus all the time now. Jesus has transformed my life and become my best friend. I've chosen to live my life for Him. I will always love Hero because he's a reminder of this gift."

What I've come to realize about our wilderness times is that no matter who we are or what we're suffering, every wilderness has a name—and it's been the same name throughout the ages. The name of every wasteland we will ever experience is called *choice*. Not because we have chosen it, for none of us can choose or control all our circumstances. But all of us can choose to abide in the peace of Christ through them.

The truth is that out of His love and mercy, Christ gave His life for us so that we could live. He didn't lay down His life only to abandon us. On the contrary, "The LORD is a shelter for the oppressed, a refuge in times of trouble. Those who know your name trust in you, for you, O LORD, *have never abandoned anyone who searches for you*" (Psalm 9:9–10).

Even if we're discarded by those who promised to fill our lives with love, the Lord Himself vows to always be with us, no matter what wilderness we find ourselves lost within: "Even if my father and mother abandon me, the LORD will hold me close" (Psalm 27:10).

Thankfully, when it comes to our King's acceptance of us, it doesn't matter how we feel. All that matters is what is true. Our feelings can change from moment to moment, yet the truth of His Word and how He feels about us remain the same forever: "Trust yourself to the God who made you, for he will never fail you" (1 Peter 4:19).

Our King loves us unconditionally. To prove it, He's prepared a way for us to live in His house—filled with His love—forever: "God showed how much he loved us by sending his only Son into the world so that we might have eternal life through him. This is real love.… We know how much God loves us, and we have put our trust in him. *God is love,* and all who live in love live in God, and God lives in them" (1 John 4:9–10, 16).

We might lose sight of Jesus, but He *never* loses sight of us.

Friend, there is no wilderness of despair so vast that His hope cannot reach. There is no depth of pain so deep that His peace cannot find. There is no anguish of soul so great that His love cannot conquer. There is no place you can go where His saving grace cannot redeem you. All that He is and all that He offers to you is as near as your lips and your heart. *Anyone* who calls on the name of the Lord will be saved.

Our loving and merciful Father is always standing by, ready to lead us home.

Editor's Note: Read more about Sue in "Friendship," chapter 20 of Kim's book *Bridge Called Hope*.

THE WARRIOR

13

THE CHOICE

Her Crown for His Sword

It was late evening, and I was still working on a laptop in my secluded lookout on the crest at our ranch. Long gone was the golden glow of the setting sun's last rays. In its place, as if on a timeless theater stage, the dark sky had silently ushered in the twinkling glow of countless stars. Hardly aware of the beauty above me, I was captivated by a scene playing out in my mind. Surging forth like a primeval play was the image of a solitary woman surrounded by dark shapes, preparing to make a mortal choice...

The woman stood in the dim light. Her hair was blowing gently in an unseen breeze. Her feet were wide apart, her weight balanced evenly. She narrowed her eyes on the objects before her: a golden crown in her left hand and a silver sword in her right. She repeatedly glanced at first one item, then the other.

Suddenly, purposefully, she looked straight up.

Evil curses began filling the air. "You *can't* do it. You're too weak!" hissed one shadow. "You deserve to stay where you are!" cried another. "Don't do it! Don't *do* it!"

Seemingly oblivious to the voices, the woman lowered her chin and blinked. As she studied the crown again, sliding the forefinger of her left hand along the edge of an emerald, she smiled. Voices seethed all around her: "Yes! Yes, you love this!" She turned the crown upside down and examined its rim, the golden sphere that for so many years had rested upon her head.

The woman's smile slowly twisted into a dark frown.

Her next thoughts came from the deepest corner of her heart, from a place of pain and rushing awareness, so powerful that they filled the air as if she were speaking aloud:

"This exquisite crown would guarantee me the admiration, acceptance, and honor of men. It would also unite me to a life of serving... myself. By choosing it, I would be bound to a public life of praise and a private life of purposeless, selfish ambition. I would reign as a princess, rule my own life, and become my own god." Evil murmurs of agreement and praise rose around her like blinding black smoke.

The woman turned her attention to the sword in her other hand.

"This ordinary sword would promise a life of ongoing confrontation, rejection, and ridicule by many. It would also bond me to a life of serving others before myself. By choosing it, I would become a servant of the Most High King, bound to a public life of allegiance to Him and a private life of love, peace, joy, and eternal purpose."

A slow smile spread across the woman's beautiful lips. Her smile increased in brilliance until it split into honest, energetic laughter.

Holding what once held her, the woman extended her left arm. Then she opened her hand and let the crown fall.

Wicked and foul screams shrieked all around her. "No! No! *Noooooo!*"

The crown dropped heavily. It bounced on its lower rim and turned over onto its glittering side. The golden sphere rolled in a lazy semicircle, its faceted gems flashing in multicolored radiance, until it finally came to a stop.

The woman gazed at the dazzling former prison that she had lived most of her days building, rationalizing, defending...and worshiping. Demonic witnesses held their breath.

What she saw for the first time was just how much of her life had been spent enslaved within the crown's indulgent golden bars. Around her, more vile blasphemies spewed out of the darkness. Staring at the lustrous hell she had once embraced, she smiled again. This time it was a knowing grin of righteous justice.

She realized that as long as she wore this crown, she was already dead.

But it didn't have to be so. This was not her end. It was her beginning.

Her great enemy had used this decadent fortress of selfishness to encircle and captivate her thoughts, control her actions, and nearly destroy her life. She knew that in all fairness the moment had come to return the favor. With a determination for retribution reserved only for demonic hordes, she breathed through clenched teeth, "It's time for payback!"

The woman lifted her foot over the crown and stamped it again and again, crushing the crown into what it had always been—a radiant pile of trash.

A hideous chorus of screams shrieked all around her. The darkness that veiled the woman instantly began to burn away in the presence of a growing light that emanated from her chest. Right before the narrowed evil eyes that encircled her, the woman was being transformed.

After a last devastating blow with her foot, she seemed satisfied with the complete destruction of what had nearly destroyed her. Pleased there was no surviving portion of the crown that could be resurrected, the woman stepped over it. She pushed back her hair, wiped her brow, and looked up once more.

The woman raised the point of her sword as high as she could, drew in a massive breath, and shouted in a voice loud enough for the heavens to hear, "For the King alone!"

Instantly white-hot light pulsed from the center of her torso. Its blinding flash scattered the black swarm around her. The brilliant glow spread like an accelerated sunrise through her entire being. Once the radiance reached her perimeters, it began to build. As it continued to gather intensity, a deafening crackle filled the air. What looked like her skin began to fracture as if it were sunbaked mud. Each crack grew wider until her covering was pulled so tight that it strained to hold her.

Finally, in a series of sharp snaps, her exterior exploded in a rancid hail of filmy gray scales. Gone were the slimy, man-made attempts at creating beauty. Gone was the pride; gone was the fear; gone was the selfish justification. Gone was the *princess*.

In her place stood a warrior.

14

THE SMILE

A Solitary Strand of Hope

Several years ago someone I love very much shared with me an account from her life, one that has since changed mine.

On a five-day canoe trip through the Okefenokee Swamp on the Georgia-Florida border, Misheal and I paddled down what seemed a long-forgotten waterway. We set out, two ponytailed explorers, with several dry bags filled with our gear and enough food to last the length of our trip. Because the swamp is a wildlife reserve, it is also a haven for thousands of American alligators. We entered their black-water kingdom cupped in a sixteen-foot canoe. Our conversation meandered with the same unhurried luxury as the river upon which we traveled.

I encouraged my friend's heart with the news that no one venturing into the Okefenokee has ever been seriously injured by an alligator, in part because all adventurers are required to paddle a specified distance of up to twelve miles a day to reach a series of elevated platforms. The raised floors were designed to give travelers a safe place to pitch their tents at night. Each wooden campsite rises several feet out of the water and above the reach of cruising alligators. Twenty feet long by twenty-eight feet wide, these stages are among the few places in the swamp where the gators cannot climb.

Having made this trip before, I knew the inhabitants of this wilderness grow to approximately fourteen feet in length and have a mouth lined with dozens of prehistoric-looking teeth. Backing those teeth is a set of jaws that have produced one of the strongest bite pressures ever recorded. With that bit of information firmly in mind, combined with the understanding that these ancient predators are primarily nocturnal hunters, locating our platform before dark each day was always a high priority. Actually, as fearsome as they look and truly are in their habitat, most alligators are very shy. Other than those who've been fed by tourists, they do not naturally seek interaction with humans.

Since it was my friend's first trip to the swamp, I wanted her to be in the front of our canoe so she could see, without distraction, the matchless beauty this unique setting has to offer. Selfishly, I also wanted to be the steersman in the back of our boat so I could see her reaction to each miraculous wonder God had stowed within this hidden place.

Perhaps lulled by the magnificent, embracing arms of the cypress trees overhead or the intense privacy of utter silence, it was within this sanctuary that Misheal's remarkable story began to emerge.

After several days of navigating the swamp and many alligator encounters, we paddled on in silent synchronization. Our words wandered as aimlessly as the brilliant blue dragonflies that danced around us. Eventually our dialogue moved toward the difficulties of our childhoods. Once we rounded this conversational bend, I observed a change in my dark-haired friend. Her back and upper body subtly stiffened, and her voice thinned. Clearly, our words were nearing something very painful in her past.

My mind extrapolated from these changes the image of a frightened child. The little girl I envisioned had her knees drawn up tightly, her face buried between them. With her slender arms wrapped around her legs, she squeezed with all her might. This cringing child was trying to fit into a smaller space than she physically occupied.

I realized that for most of her life, Misheal had hidden in plain sight. Yet on this day in our canoe, with every slow, courageous word she spoke, fear started to release its awful grip on the little girl it controlled. Like the pure white water lilies that our boat glided through, the beautiful grown woman before me began to unclench, breathe deeply, and open, petal by flawless petal, into a precious, perfect bloom.

With her black ponytail brushing against the deeply tanned skin of her back, Misheal shared about her troubled and violent home life. Things in her outwardly perfect family became so tumultuous and threatening that—without warning—the house of cards came crashing down. I continued to listen in ever-deepening sorrow as she recounted how her life and mine were joined by the experience of having our families torn apart.

Finally her home life became so terrifying, so dangerous, that law enforcement officials intervened. At the age of fifteen, she was taken away from the only home she had ever known. In the blurring aftermath she was literally dropped into a new home, with new parents and new surroundings many miles away. My friend lost her beloved mother, her family, her home, her confidant, her friends, her school, her peer group, her neighborhood, and all that was familiar.

In a single day she lost *everything*.

It was upon this unfamiliar skeleton that she was expected to build a new life. This devastating event took place in the winter, in the middle of the school year. As if nothing had happened, the following Monday she was trundled off to a new high school. Completely alone and burdened with an armload of books, she walked down hallways she'd never seen before.

My friend conceded that going to a new school is hard for anyone. But since it was already halfway through the year, all the peer groups were already tightly knit and definitely not in need of a new, broken member. Misheal was alone.

Overwhelmed by a crippling combination of acute shyness and mind-numbing grief, Misheal didn't have enough emotional strength even to try to build new friendships. Without question, this was the darkest season of her life. She was caving in, and no one seemed to notice or care.

In the canoe Misheal paused to look up into the elegant canopy of cypress limbs. Ten-foot Spanish moss streamers wafted in the lazy breeze as if encouraging her to continue speaking. Misheal seemed to be looking for something, perhaps the right words, as she pondered their swaying invitation. Finally her shoulders lifted as she took a deep breath and steeled herself to press through her pain.

Misheal recalled how, at that time in her life, she had been reduced by her anguish to little more than a hollow shell. Too weak to cry out for help, she simply cried. What was most deeply etched into her memory was that at the end of her first day in the new school, she realized no one had spoken to her. No one had even looked at her.

No one.

One day in the new school became two, then a week, then a month. Still, not one person engaged her in conversation or even looked her way. She was dying inside, and no one cared or even knew who she was.

Eventually, two months went by, and still not one person had spoken to her; not one person had even looked into her face—*not one*!

That's when Misheal made her decision. It was time for her misery to end. She was sitting in the back row of her fourth-period math class when she came to this conclusion. She reasoned that no human being should suffer like this. In order to make the hurt in her heart stop, it made sense to her that this would only be possible…if she just made her *heart* stop.

At that grave moment she decided to go home and end her life.

Once Misheal crossed that bridge emotionally, it all seemed so logical. Her anguish would finally cease. She would be released from her pain. She found unexpected peace in this choice. She knew that among these merciless halls, she was nothing more than a dark-haired phantom. Although highly intelligent, she didn't feel valuable enough to engage others in conversation. Though stunning in appearance, she didn't feel appealing enough for others to even see. She would end her life and never be found in these forsaken corridors again.

No one will ever know that I died, she thought, *because, truly, no one ever knew that I lived.*

With her decision in place, Misheal allowed her attention to wander to the intermittent showers outside her classroom window. She wondered if the gray weather was mourning with her. Then the bell rang, ending the last math class she would ever know. She gathered her books and looked up at the classroom doorway as she walked beneath its tired frame. It felt strange to think she would never pass through this doorway again. Even more strange was that this revelation did not make her feel sad.

Misheal was joined in the hallway by a thousand other milling students seeking to steer through the same river of humanity. Carrying her books close to her chest, as she had for weeks, she drifted unseen through the churning mass.

Without warning, she was hit hard by a boy on the losing end of a shoving match. The force of the impact slammed her knees against the floor. Her armload of books splattered across the filthy tiles, hitting with such violence that they bounced into open, crumpled pages.

Careless feet marched over everything that only moments ago had been held safe in her arms. Tossed about beneath the dirty stampede were her composition books, pens, assignments, and notes. From her knees she watched in stunned silence as each item was stamped with the grimy, wet tread marks of the herd that trampled over them. She felt just like her broken, trodden things, cast beneath the uncaring feet of the world.

No one reached out to her. No one offered to help her up. No one seemed to care. Believing this was an accurate picture of her life, she shuffled through the stampede and, piece by piece, retrieved the soiled and tattered remnants of her things.

The incident and the callous response by her schoolmates confirmed to Misheal that she was making the right decision. Her prison of shyness was the only fragile wall that kept her tears from spilling over into this cold, indifferent corridor.

Trying to outrun her urge to cry, she gathered her belongings as quickly as she could and began walking. Glancing up, she noticed that a blond girl on the other side of the hallway was watching. Apparently she had seen the entire episode. Their eyes locked. Misheal was certain that at any minute the blond girl would burst out laughing or point and jeer.

Yet she did neither.

Instead, from the opposite side of the hallway, intense blue eyes held deep brown eyes. As Misheal walked, the gap between them closed.

Finally, just as the two girls passed, the blond girl did something unexpected.

She smiled.

Misheal followed the warmth of that smile as far as the rotation of her neck would bear. She couldn't believe it. Was the blond girl *really* looking at her? What did she mean by that smile? Was it sincere? Was it born out of care—or pity? On the bus ride home, these questions plagued her crushed heart.

Finally the dilapidated school-bus doors opened, and the broken girl stepped out. As she walked the short distance to her new home, she reaffirmed her commitment to her earlier decision. This was the only way to make her pain cease. It was the only way she knew to find lasting peace.

Inside the house Misheal gathered the implements she would need to carry out her intentions. With everything in hand she went to the place she had chosen and prepared to proceed with her plan. Then she knelt on the floor.

Cradled in our canoe on the Okefenokee, my friend stopped her account.

I don't think I realized until that moment that I had been holding my breath, as perhaps the angels that surrounded a hopeless young woman on that devastating day had done.

I watched in heavy silence as my dear friend laid her paddle across her thighs. We had left the protective overhang of the cypress trees and were now passing through a floating prairie. Within this rare place, suspended on the surface of the water, grew a lovely garden of grasses, sedge, and wildflowers. In sharp contrast to my friend's terrible tale and as if to cheer her on, bright yellow flowers pressed around our boat as we passed through a narrow gap.

Misheal turned slightly. To me, her profile was a flawless masterpiece of courage and grace. Slowly, softly, she pressed through her self-imposed silence and explained how she was poised to end her life. Locked momentarily in a position of self-destruction, images flashed before her tightly shut eyes. The one picture that was most relentless was the warm smile given by a complete stranger.

Held fast in the extreme awareness of the moment, Misheal's whole body began to shake. Again the smile came back to her mind. At the speed of light, her thoughts streamed through an unexpected sequence: maybe it meant something, maybe it was real, maybe there was *one* person in the world who cared enough about her to offer a smile. *Maybe...*

Her drawn body withdrew in a sobbing, nauseating gush of emotion. She collapsed on the floor and held herself as she cried. The solitary strand of hope that she clung to was the light within that single smile.

With her anguish released in a torrent, finally there were no more tears to accompany her sobs. All that was left were deep, empty convulsions. It was only when she was completely spent that she slowly summoned herself from the floor.

She had to know. If the smile was a hoax, she would follow through with her plans tomorrow. She would wait *one* more day.

The next afternoon at school, as the bell rang to herald the end of another math class, Misheal scooped up her books and again stepped into the crowded hallway. Fueled by heightened anticipation, she carried her books nearly under her chin. Scanning the multitude, she heard a child's voice calling inside her chest, "Are you there? Are you really there? Is there *one*...who might care for me?"

None of the faces that moved past her looked familiar. Now, nearly on her tippytoes, she cried out with her eyes, *Where are you?*

She continued to search the throng as she drew closer to her destination. Her throat tightened. Her one thread of hope was fading.

Misheal stopped momentarily in front of the doorway of her final class. She knew that if she stepped through, it was over. This was it. Her blood chilled as if it were turning to ice, crackling in from her extremities. She couldn't move.

One last time she glanced down the hallway.

Suddenly, from around a corner in the corridor, the blond girl appeared. She was looking over heads too.

As if drawn by a magnetic pull, bright blue eyes found dark brown eyes. A second time the blond girl's face brightened into a warm smile. Again their gazes held as the stranger walked closer, then past, then out of sight.

Once more the broken girl received a single breath of life in her gasping world.

One day became two. The blond girl kept smiling. Two days became a week. Weeks became a month. Two months went by.

As she told the story, the adult woman in the front of my canoe seemed to transform back into that expectant, hopeful young girl. Misheal said she knew that if she could just hold on until that space between fourth and fifth periods, she would be okay. One smile a day was enough encouragement for her to keep choosing to get out of bed. One smile a day was enough for her to keep fighting for her life.

This went on every day until the school year ended. Turning around to look at me, Misheal said, "One smile a day saved my life. One smile a day is what gave me the courage to hold on to hope just a little longer… until the day that I met the Author of hope, my Jesus."

With that, Misheal smiled at me—a deep smile that I will never see the same way again.

"School came and went," Misheal said. "The blond girl and I never even knew each other's names. We never even met. She will never know how God used the simple gift she gave me. She will never know that she saved my life with nothing more than a smile."

Nothing more than a smile.

The power in this phrase has changed everything about what I yield to God. Misheal has been faithful about passing on the gift that was given to her. By sharing the story of her life, she has forever changed mine…and hopefully yours.

SOMETHING WE CAN GIVE

A warrior answers God's call to give Him
whatever she can, no matter how small.

It's true that God will use whatever we give.

It's not up to us to understand how He will use our gifts. Our responsibility is solely to be faithful and obedient to His urging to give them. He is the King who turns a few barley loaves and two fish into a feast for thousands. Our gifts might seem incredibly small and insignificant. Yet when we step forward in faith and place them in the hands of our Lord, *everything* changes! He is the One who can transform our meager offerings into something amazing, something incredible, even something life changing.

From our perspective what we have might seem meaningless. Most have asked, "Who am I, and what do I really have to give?" Because of this mind-set, it's easy to fall into the belief that we don't have much to give so why give anything at all?

Friend, when we give God nothing, that's *exactly* what we can expect to happen in our own hearts and the hearts of those He has called us to serve.

But when we give Him something—even a little thing—we open the door for our God to do incredible things. Our simple actions reveal that we're taking steps of faith. Each step builds greater trust. And just like the little boy who ran through the crowd of five thousand, we prove by our actions that we believe our King can take our "sack lunch" and do something *amazing*.

In such a moment we become just like Moses standing on the edge of the Red Sea waving a stick. God parted an entire sea because Moses wielded a stick over it! But it wasn't the stick that parted the sea. Moses expected, he believed, that his King was going to act. And, boy, *did* He.

God will use whatever you give. He is God. He doesn't require our gifts, talents, and abilities. He requires our hearts. For it is from a heart that *wants* to serve Him that He splits oceans. Someone far wiser than I once said, "God does not call the equipped—He equips those He calls." Trust me, our King does not need what we value in our worldly way of thinking. He has no use for our physical beauty, knowledge, strength, power, position, skills, or money. Yet He can—and does—use all those things when they are offered to Him with a willing and sincere heart.

No matter what God calls us to do, fear should have no place in our lives. We can relax in the fact that our King's call on each of our lives will never lead us beyond His ability to provide for us. It is our King alone who makes *whatever* we hold in our hands a force to be used for His purpose and glory. But that force can be applied only when we *give it to Him.*

Moses gave God a stick (Exodus 14:15–31), Gideon gave Him clay jars and torches (Judges 7), David gave a sling (1 Samuel 17), a widow gave two mites (Luke 21:1–4), a boy gave his sack lunch (John 6:1–13), and Paul gave his imprisonment (Acts 28:30–31).

What has God already equipped *you* with to give back to Him?

We may never see the purpose of our gifts. But the Lord sees all time, all history, all at once. He views the entire panorama. We see only a tiny picture full of puzzle pieces. Within that picture each of us represents a single puzzle piece. And one thing about puzzles is that they usually come with "inny" and "outy" pieces. This makes me visualize introverts and extroverts, leaders and followers. Another fact I've realized is that it's impossible—the picture absolutely cannot work—if any two pieces are the *same*. Friend, it is our uniqueness that allows us to fit together to make a clear picture.

We were created to interlock with those God has called around us. Only when our true focus is on our King can we join together in perfect unity, thus creating a flawless image. And when this image is viewed from a distance, it will reflect the attributes of our Lord.

This analogy also extends to music. No one would want to listen to a symphony where all the instruments were the same and each played exactly the same note over and over. It is the harmonious blending of scores of instruments playing their unique tones—together—that makes the music beautiful. We shouldn't judge, despair, or measure our differences. We should *celebrate* them.

We each have our own gifts, our own tones, our own shapes, our own voices to be offered up to our King. All of us can present something that He can transform for His glory. It doesn't matter how old or how young we are. It makes no difference if we are broken or weak. Even for those whose lives are severely restricted, nothing in this world can take away their ability to pray. As long as our hearts continue to beat, we have *something* we can give.

Whether our gift be as small as a handful of flowers, a phone call, a hug, an e-mail, a plate of cookies, a card, a handshake, a letter, a kiss, a wink—or even something as simple as a smile—God will use whatever we give.

We cannot begin to guess what He's going to do with our gifts—and we will never find out until we choose to give them.

Friend, our King is calling you to give Him something to be used for His glory. Today, what might be *your* smile?

15

THE FALL

A Beautiful Sound

It was July, and my friend Joan and I were on a small boat. We had just left a scenic harbor located on the tip of the Homer Spit in Alaska. Taxiing out into the paradise of Kachemak Bay, I was entranced by the enormous beauty that soared around us. The bay was nearly encircled by the snowy white crown of the Kenai mountain range that towered above us. While we were humming across the water, the din of the boat's outboard motor overtook our conversation. The happy drone provided an unexpected opportunity to reflect on many things...especially how much I cherished this woman.

Our powerful friendship had been forged more than twenty years earlier, primarily in the Cascade mountains and on the ski tracks of Mount Bachelor. During my fledgling pursuit of a new sport, it was Joan who imparted to me a unique love of Nordic skiing. She chose to look past my initial ineptitude and focus instead on my desire. By doing so, she fueled my passion to develop as a skate skier.

Joan was a multi-Olympian in biathlon. It was from her warehouse of equipment that she pulled out my first set of skis and poles, gear that I cherish to this day. In return I gave her as honest a friendship as I could muster and what I hoped would be a reflection of Jesus Christ.

Over the years our friendship grew deep and profound roots. Traveling from race to race across the United States, I wrote to her. Traveling from country to country around the world, she wrote back. As often as we were able, we trained together—she being the teacher, I the student.

In part because of her tutelage, I earned a position on the Central Oregon Community College ski team, then nationally acclaimed. Though small, this team was fierce. We dominated all other Northwest teams and went on to compete in the U.S. Collegiate Ski and Snowboard Association National Championships. Pitted against nearly one hundred other nationally ranked Nordic teams, our men's squad earned gold, and our women's team earned bronze.

After graduating from college, I felt I was just beginning to fully grasp my love for skate skiing and decided to follow Joan's lead into the world of biathlon. During this time, while skating in late December, our training took us into the wilderness around a high, frozen lake. After we circumvented its crunchy edge, our conversation turned toward faith. It was here, while coming around the north end of Todd Lake, that she heard the loving voice of Jesus calling her name. Kneeling side by side on our skis, with her hand in mine, we prayed.

Through tears of release, Joan surrendered her heart to the King of kings.

Because of that decision, our friendship deepened to a level far beyond what we'd known before. Bound by our Lord, we prayed for each other daily. Even when separated by travels, distance, or time zones, our hearts were linked. On many occasions I was jarred awake in the early morning hours by an urgent need to pray for Joan. Later I would learn that at nearly the same time, she was in peril and narrowly escaped. Our long-distance prayers for each other gave us a connection that challenged logic.

Yet in the years that followed, our beautiful friendship gradually began to fade. Fed by a constant breeze of pride, our unique camaraderie started to tatter like a flag left to flutter in the weather too long. Perceived offense by perceived offense, poor decision by poor decision, a barrier grew between us.

Looking back, I'm filled with immense sorrow over the realization that I could have torn down that wall at any time. I could have asked for her forgiveness and confessed my faults and failings. I could have taken responsibility for my part in this breakdown.

I could have, but I didn't. I failed her. More important, I failed Jesus Christ.

I didn't take the lead in our friendship by courageously stepping forward and fighting for the truth. Instead, I chose the path of a justified coward; I simply stepped backward and avoided it. I let every excuse bend my judgment away from what I didn't want to deal with.

Yet, what was real burned deep in my chest. Truth is a light that no dark action or word can extinguish. Therefore, I couldn't find honest rest. There was nowhere in my soul I could hide my self-righteousness, pride, arrogance, and unforgiveness. No amount of waiting, ignoring, justifying, evading, or burying could hide this festering rot inside my heart.

There was only one cure. I needed to repent before my King, and then I needed to genuinely seek Joan's forgiveness and genuinely give her mine. I was accountable to make right my failings in this fractured friendship. Because I knew this was true, I alone was responsible to step toward this end.

It wasn't until my precious grandmother passed away that I found the impetus to act. While sorting through her keepsakes, I discovered a bundle of saved letters. Held together by a worn rubber band was a collection of cards that Joan had written her over the years.

After my parents' death, it was my grandmother who, even while grieving the loss of her daughter, courageously stepped forward and made a home for her three orphaned granddaughters. I lived in her home a year longer than that of my parents. Even though Joan and I were estranged, she continued to write supportive letters to my Mimi. The letters came after my grandfather had passed away and my tiny grandma was living alone. I held in my hand a gift of pure kindness, given to my Mimi when she needed it most. Joan hadn't waited for my approval. She chose instead simply to do what was right.

Kneeling among my grandmother's things, I couldn't hold back the flood of tears. Worlds collided as I crumpled to the floor. I grieved the loss of my beloved grandmother, one of the greatest pillars of love, support, and kindness I had ever known. Tears also fell for the loss of one of the greatest friendships I had ever known.

Truth landed on my heart with all the subtlety of an anvil dropping out of the sky. My grandmother was gone... Joan was not.

God is so good. His mercy and redemption are not prisoners of time. I sent Joan, my once-treasured friend, a simple letter—and so forgiveness began.

Joan's willingness to move beyond the past and her tremendous example of friendship, combined with God's great love, led both of us to choose to disassemble the wall between us. This beautiful, redemptive feat was achieved entirely through correspondence.

To my deep joy, for every letter I sent Joan, she returned the kindness—times five! Fifteen years later, after what the enemy had assumed was a fatal blow to our alliance, I now sat looking at this remarkable friend in our small water taxi as we traversed paradise itself. She was no longer a world-class athlete. She had traded that title for the deeper calling of being a world-class wife and mother of three incredible kids.

The silent years had added their touches. We were each a bit heavier and a tad more gray. Lines we'd earned from years of smiling framed our faces. And thankfully, by God's grace, we were *much* wiser.

Sitting near the railing directly behind her, I watched as she draped her arm over the side of the boat and let the seawater bounce off her palm. She turned to look at me and flashed an impish grin. I shook my head and held my hands up in a silent *Can you believe this?* gesture. She laughed and nodded in agreement.

In that moment I couldn't imagine a more beautiful and profound vision of forgiveness. But as I was soon to find out, God's imagination is *far* greater than mine.

After motoring deep into Halibut Cove, Joan and I reached our destination—a beautiful camp of small cabins that hovered over the bay. With our packs slung over our shoulders, we made our way up to bunks reserved for us. In the land of the midnight sun, we lay sprawled on our beds, talking, crying, and laughing until deep into the purple twilight. Finally, at 2 a.m., we extinguished our kerosene lantern and tried to get some rest before our glacier exploration the following dawn.

Early the next morning, under a low, gray sky, we joined a team of four other people and started to hike. Our group was led by a remarkable guide, a man of great faith and the father of five small boys.

We traveled up through an incredibly dense forest that lined the steep southwestern foothills that jutted above the bay. After hiking over a small coastal ridge, we dropped into the massive flood plain that streamed out below the Grewingk Glacier. This glacier is one of nine that drain the great Harding Icefield. At roughly a thousand square miles, the ice field is the largest of its type located entirely within the United States. The slow retreat of Grewingk Glacier left behind a vast trough, gouged out between flanking four-thousand-foot sheer ridges, giving dramatic evidence of the colossal power of moving ice.

Spectacular beauty rose to soaring heights all around us as we traversed the smooth-stoned delta. Following a serpentine trail, we moved through a thick tangle of stunted alder. After another mile we finally emerged from the bush onto a giant shoreline. Walking away from the thicket in speechless awe, our party arrived on the edge of an enormous body of water. Created by the scouring of the glacier, the lake is roughly a mile wide and several miles in length. Our guide shared that it has been measured to depths of over twelve hundred feet, further proof of the mighty force of ice on the move.

From our vantage point the lake appeared to be shaped in a vast dogleg that was pinched in the middle by a smooth ridge of granite. This feature temporarily blocked our view of the glacier's titanic face. The water was milky gray from glacial "flour"—rock so finely pulverized that, when mixed with liquid, it lightens in color, sometimes even turning white. We were informed that the water temperature was only slightly above freezing. A great flotilla of beautiful icebergs gave evidence of this truth.

Our guide beckoned us to help him haul inflatable kayaks and waterproof gear from a cache hidden in the thick alders. Everyone was needed to prepare the boats for paddling across the frozen lake to a vantage point where we could fully view the magnificent glory of the Grewingk Glacier.

As we inflated our boats, a thunderous sound pierced the frigid air. Sensing danger, everyone stopped moving and looked in the direction of the hidden glacier. Even though this gargantuan river of ice was approximately two miles away, our guide walked to the water's edge and casually drew a line in the sand. Returning to our spot on the shore, he smiled and said, "Watch. In a few minutes you'll see a mini-tsunami wash over this line."

As we continued our preparation, we heard an ominous roar echo out of the chasm. It was the sound of waves rushing toward us, crashing against the canyon walls as they came. Just as our guide had said, several moments later a series of small waves, the greatest being about three feet high, lapped up around us.

I looked across the immense gray waters in pure wonder. My mind reeled at the thought of just how *much* falling ice it took to displace this much water—this far away. Tiny needles of alarm prickled up the back of my scalp.

Though Joan and I own kayaks and are experienced paddlers, we agreed that piloting an inflatable kayak is a whole different experience. It was a bit eerie to sit down in what felt like a soft, shaky, twisty boat—in ice water. Since the prow of an inflatable kayak is longer than the back and I'm taller, I settled onto the front floor. Once I was balanced, Joan gingerly climbed into the back. With a careful push off the rocks, we were on our way.

It was intimidating to sit on the floor of the boat and know that my backside was inches below the frigid water's surface. In this soft-sided, tippy kayak, only a few inches of rubber rose above the water level to keep us safe. The flexible boat seemed much more precarious and wobbly than a hard-sided kayak. Yet after a few practice turns, we were able to gain a feel for our craft and its balance point.

In addition to our guide, our small team consisted of a husband and wife in one kayak and a mother and daughter in another. I noticed the submissive mother trying her best to make the experience a special memory for her daughter. Sadly, the dominant, spoiled teenager made it equally clear that her mother was "making" her do this. When our guide gave them a brief tutorial on how to balance, paddle, and steer, the daughter didn't even try. My sorrow for the mother was overshadowed by an ominous sense of caution. This was not a forgiving environment for selfish apathy.

After learning a few simple but sobering safety precautions, our armada of four little boats set out into the vast, milky waters.

Once we fell into a smooth paddling rhythm, I had time to process the words of our guide. In all his years he'd never lost anyone, nor had anyone fallen into the lake. He assured our group that he was practiced at his "retrieving" skills, rehearsed with other guides, and could pull victims out of the frigid water in less than a minute. This was good information to know since he'd also told us that if you go into the water, you have approximately three minutes to live.

We were forewarned that turning around in these soft kayaks was forbidden, because the shift of a single torso could pull the entire boat over. Therefore, all cameras—including mine—had to be stowed to prevent the temptation to twist around for shots. Being careful not to rotate too much, I spoke to my dear friend over my shoulder as we paddled slightly ahead of the group.

Even though I was heavily dressed in waterproof gear, it took only moments for me to notice a sharp lowering of the air temperature. My breath had transformed into white wisps that streamed back over both of my shoulders.

Drifting in an unseen current a few hundred yards to our right, a virtual parade of mammoth icebergs seemed to flaunt their spectacular beauty. Shaped by the merciless elements, each statuesque form appeared to revel in its unique display of graceful artistry.

Soon our small group crossed the expanse of the lake and approached the dogleg. Here, an audacious length of smooth, glacier-scoured granite formed a bend in the massive lake. As our guide spoke of the cataclysmic forces that had shaped this landscape, Joan and I drifted slightly beyond the stretch of granite that blocked our view of the glacier. As we looked down the mile-long hallway of rising stone, the grandeur of Grewingk Glacier came into full view.

Neither of us could speak.

We stared at the towering mass, barely hearing the voice of our guide. Pure awe overwhelmed us. A solid wall of ice soared three hundred feet straight up and spanned more than a mile in width. This was the mighty terminus of thirteen miles of moving ice.

Having finished his description, our guide began to lead the other two boats toward Joan and me. Suddenly sounds like sharp cracks of lightning thundered in a deafening series of booms from the glacier.

Joan and I turned and watched in astonishment as the leading edge of the glacier began to collapse. Walls of ice as high as a thirty-story building were falling!

In what looked like slow motion, more than one thousand horizontal feet of the face began to shear away. Rushing down and forward, the titanic slab of ice hit the water and exploded into a massive plume of ice crystals.

From it rose a wave that we could see even at our distance.

Our guide, coming out from behind the granite, saw only the last phase of the fall.

"Oh my gosh!" he shouted. "Oh my gosh! *Oh my gosh!* In my twelve years as a guide here, this is the largest fall I've ever seen. Oh my gosh! Come, everyone, follow me. We must get away from the shore. Quickly, quickly! We must get out into the deep water. Follow me *now!*"

In a rapid series of strokes, Joan and I were fifty yards offshore. We turned our boat to see if the others were with us. The married couple seemed to be managing well. But the mother-daughter team in the other boat was struggling to move forward at all. The daughter appeared to rebel at her mother's insistent urging and simply refused to paddle.

Looking back at the glacier, I watched in rising alarm as icebergs half a mile away were lifted into the air by the rushing swell passing under them. The daughter's poor behavior had moved from annoying…to deadly.

With cool authority covering his rising distress, the guide swiftly paddled back to the imperiled family and implored them to work together. As precious time was rapidly running out, the guide pointed his paddle blade at the girl and firmly stated, "*You,* paddle with her *right now*! You're in a dangerous place, and you must move! Follow me *right now*!"

To everyone's great relief, the girl sobered up and responded. Quickly we were all reunited in deeper water.

Hastily turning toward the approaching wave, our guide said, "Do not try to outrun the waves—you can't. By attempting to, you will be overtaken and capsized. Instead, do the opposite of what you feel. *Turn directly into them* and paddle *through* them. Everyone's going to be fine. It's time for us to enjoy the show."

Joan and I turned our kayak perpendicular to the advancing wave and held a ready position for what might happen next.

Having relocated in the main channel, we were surrounded by the fringe of the iceberg field. The wave was fifty yards away, then forty, then thirty. As it approached, the icebergs directly in front of us rose ominously.

Twenty yards. Ten yards.

Our boat began to rise. Joan and I paddled steadily forward as the ice all around us lifted. The first wave rolled underneath us.

As we looked at the shore where we'd just been, the shallow granite reef forced the wave to rise to perhaps a dozen feet, then curl over like an enormous ocean breaker. As it did so, it carried truck-size blocks of ice onto the rocks. Crushed by the weight of the waves hitting the stone, the ice blocks exploded into countless pieces.

As bigger icebergs were fractured and their weight and buoyancy displaced, the immediate imbalance made them quickly roll over. In doing so they threw off their own dislodged members in a spectacular and terrifying hail of enormous ice blocks. Intensified by the granite reef, the wave easily carried the truck-size ice chunks up into the alder groves *above* the rocks.

Had we stayed in what appeared to be the relative safety of the shallow reef, we all would have been crushed to death.

With each boat and paddler accounted for, our guide directed our attention back in the direction of the glacier. Another sizable wave was rushing toward us. Again I watched in mouth-agape awe as massive icebergs bobbed like toys in the tub of a raucous child. In another dazzling display of pure power, more ice was pulverized against the reef, flung through the air, and deposited far beyond the shoreline into the alders. By the end of the event, we had survived not one wave—but *seven*.

By now we could see that fully one third of the glacier's immense face had been sheared away. There, beneath the older, dilapidated facade, lay something beautiful, something extraordinary.

Where once stood an ancient, deteriorating mass of dirt-encrusted ice now towered a vertical wall of deep blue so intense that I didn't know such a rich color even existed. It had been there all along. This remarkable color had been buried beneath years of rubble that had slowly piled on from above. It wasn't until the crusty exterior was broken off that the true inner beauty was revealed.

Later in the day, while we paddled back to our starting point, my King's perspective of what we had encountered began to sink in.

I had just witnessed what genuine forgiveness looks like.

Forgiveness is not passive. It isn't only a feeling we cast toward others who've hurt us. Real forgiveness is an *action*.

The ultimate release from any hardship can be found in the same direction every time. Our help will always come, not from running *away* from our troubles, but by running *toward* our King.

Smiling to myself, I realized the extraordinary, laserish, intense blue that lay hidden deep within the glacier could have come to light only through the shearing off of the soiled crust. Our friendships also have this remarkable potential, but few choose to work through the hard "crust" to find it. Revealing this rare inner quality isn't easy, but it *is* worth the risk. If forgiveness requires a painful "shearing" to reveal the deep beauty of my King's purpose, I no longer wish to cling to my yucky crust. I choose to let it go.

While carefully paddling back through the icebergs, I was roused out of my thoughts by an unfamiliar sound. It was as if the very water itself were snapping. With care, I glanced around to determine what was happening. I noticed that we were paddling through slush, the crushed remnants of what was once the face of the glacier. Ice that had been imprisoned by immeasurable compression for nearly a thousand years was now free. As it was released into the water, it began to decompress in a vast and astonishing chorus of clicks, pops, and snaps, like the echo of an infinite bowl of Rice Krispies. I couldn't help thinking that the newly freed ice was so grateful that it was *laughing*. It was a beautiful sound.

As I paddled with my dear friend in our flimsy kayak deep in the Alaskan wilderness, I continued to process all that had happened. In trying to fathom what I'd seen and heard, my mind connected the dots to a favorite old song by my friend Geoff Moore. The lyrics began to stream through my soul:

> The heart of a proud man breaking
> The cry of a sinner seeking truth
> The beat that your heart is making
> The moment that true love crashes through
> It's a beautiful sound

It's a beautiful sound
When the walls come crashing down
And the chains fall to the ground
And the song we sing
Is the song of the redeemed
Of the lost who now are found
It's a beautiful sound

Facing the Waves

A true warrior forgives. She answers her
King's call to follow Him by steering
straight into her trials and driving right
through them.

Forgiveness is a purposeful decision to let go of our years of rubble. Healing happens when we choose to honestly release the record of wrongs trapped within our hearts. When we do, the walls of our ugly justification collapse into oblivion in a thundering roar.

Yet releasing our personal dam is only the first step. The instant we let go of our walls, the waves of challenge *will* come.

Whether the swells that rush toward us are annoying or terrifying, our decision to forgive another will almost always be immediately challenged by feelings of "They haven't changed," "They're not sorry," "They don't really care," and "They're still getting their barbs in." We've all experienced waves that rush our way to capsize our newfound freedom.

Like the conflicted mother and daughter at Grewingk Glacier, we have to *want* to work together to paddle out of the danger zone. Every time the waves of confrontation rise to challenge my new forgiveness, I hear them disparage, "See! They *didn't*... They *haven't*... They *won't*..." I must choose to paddle through them by proclaiming, "Yeah, but Jesus did! So I will!"

Forgiveness is rarely a singular action but rather a process. In most situations we will need to forgive again and again. Rest in the assurance that repeating waves of anger and negativity that rush our way will only serve to wash away any resentment still lingering within our hearts. It's these waves that come from our enemy *after* we forgive that help us choose to *continue* to forgive.

Likewise, if we try to outrun the swells of challenge, we will eventually be overtaken and destroyed by them. It's only when we choose to turn toward these waves and paddle *through* them that we'll fully embrace our choice to remain free from the prison of unforgiveness.

When we purpose to continually abide in a new mind frame, we pass through the threshold of what was once our prison and into our future of liberty. It's in this place that we fully know freedom, the beautiful sovereignty that Jesus Christ purchased for us long ago. He is our only true example, and He forgives each of us, not because we deserve it, but simply because we ask.

Genuine forgiveness does *not* depend upon another's response. It is based on truth—the truth that Christ has forgiven us. Whether others respond well to our desire for reconciliation—or completely reject it—is irrelevant. What *is* relevant is that we choose to be obedient and follow the example of our Lord.

In this life many times we'll feel the onslaught of unbearable waves. Though it might not seem like it at the moment, when we face impossible seasons of stress—when the waves are too big, the icebergs too close, and the environment too severe—our King will *always* provide a way of escape. In Him, "everything is possible" (Matthew 19:26).

Many things happened that day on the lake that didn't seem coincidental. Joan and I were the only ones who saw the complete fall. I believe it was meant for *only* us to see. The Lord gave us a visual example, a covenant, of what we had already chosen to do in our hearts. Once the wall of ice came crashing down, not one wave—but seven—rampaged toward us. Each seemed to carry its own unique intent to inflict havoc and challenge our new position.

While pondering this one day, a Scripture passage emerged in my heart: "Then Peter came to him and asked, 'Lord, how often should I forgive someone who sins against me? Seven times?' 'No!' Jesus replied, *'seventy times seven!'* " (Matthew 18:21–22). The sooner we learn how to forgive, the smoother and more peaceful this journey through life becomes. We should be as quick and comfortable with choosing to forgive as we are with choosing to blink.

Friend, it's not hard—it's a choice. Since we have been forgiven, we *can* forgive. God's love is so strong that if we let it flow through us, it will crash down *all* our walls of unforgiveness.

Thank God, because He forgives completely, we're released to completely forgive.

Editor's Note: Read more about Geoff Moore and his music at www.geoffmoore.com.

16

THE SCAR

A Purpose for Every Wound

She was introduced to me as Angela. She'd come to our ranch as part of a high school incentive program for girls who were flunking their classes. What struck me was how so much sorrow could emanate from such a diminutive girl. It was exactly *because* of her sadness that I chose her out of the half-dozen girls in the group that day to work with.

Years of ranch life have taught me that the fastest way to get to know people is to work with them. Rarely do I have prior knowledge of what resides inside the hearts of those who make their way up our hill. My staff and I have discovered that a few minutes of working alongside our guests before they ride is a remarkable way for them to express stress, relax, and begin to trust. This often becomes the key that opens the great vault doors that guard the heart. It's also during this time of leaning into the harness together that my team and I have the opportunity to pour into every young heart just how much each one is needed, appreciated, and loved.

After it was established that Angela would work with me, we walked away from the group toward our waiting chore. Once sequestered from the other girls, her beautiful Hispanic features appeared even more hollow and diminished. The tiny, dark-skinned girl followed my steps without saying a word. I slowed my pace and turned toward her, hoping to begin a conversation. Angela immediately dropped her head, blocking my view of her face. Before she hid from me, however, I noticed something else: her eyes appeared listless, almost dead. The contrast between this girl's lovely features and her lifeless countenance was startling. I felt as if I were ushering a child of glass. I sensed that at any moment she might shatter into a pile of irreparable shards.

Grooming a quiet horse was an appropriate job for a girl projecting such emotional weakness. I chose Teva, an amiable palomino-mustang cross. This docile mare had a gentle nature and was the smallest horse on the ranch.

After tying Teva in a semiprivate area, I retrieved a brush bucket. Standing side by side, Angela and I began to groom our placid mare. Trying to open the door between us, I asked Angela many simple questions. Her answers were brief and emotionless. During our minimal conversation, I was surprised to learn that she was sixteen. She was so tiny she could've easily passed for a twelve-year-old.

With brush in hand I continued to explore my new friend. After each of my gentle inquiries, she politely answered with a voice even smaller than her stature.

"Do you live in Bend?" I asked.

"Uh-huh."

"Has your family lived in the area for very long?"

She thought for a moment. "Well…not really." I sensed this question exposed a conflict.

"Do you live with your mom and dad?" I gently prodded.

"Well, I used to live with my mom…but we got in a fight, and she kicked me out." Her deep brown eyes never left Teva as she continued to brush.

My heart clenched with concern. "Baby, where are you living now?"

Angela's hesitation alerted me that I was getting close to her wounding. I glanced at her smooth, dark face and noticed a tightening between her brows. Without looking up, she replied, "My best friend invited me to live with her. It was okay for a while. I liked it a lot…until her husband tried to have sex with me. I knew that wasn't right, so I left. I moved in with some other people…but I can tell they don't really want me." She paused for a moment as if to convince herself again that this was really happening. "I don't know… I'm not sure what I'm going to do."

I felt so heavy, so deflated by what this little girl was going through. I reeled back to the days when I was sixteen and all the things I worried about. Being *homeless* certainly wasn't one of them! Without thinking, I stumbled on. "Girl, what about your dad? Can you live with him?" Hoping to add emphasis to my compassion, I turned to look at her.

I wasn't prepared for what I saw next.

Angela placed her left hand on Teva's golden back to steady herself. She took a deep breath and, just for an instant, closed her eyes. Like ice trying to withstand more pressure than its brittle surface can bear, my little glass girl was cracking beneath the weight of her emotions.

Angela's dark lashes fell as her gaze plummeted. Her beautiful brown face paled as if overshadowed by ghosts she wanted to conceal. She fought for control. I watched her tiny nostrils flare repeatedly, proclaiming that tears were imminent. Her physical reaction warned me that what was about to cross her lips was intensely painful.

In that moment my prayer was little more than *Jesus…wisdom!*

The brush in Angela's right hand began to shake. She glanced at me briefly to see if I'd noticed. I had. It was over, and she knew it. Her attempt to hide had failed. Now all that was left was an emotionally exposed little girl standing in an unknown land before an unknown woman.

She was naked, alone, and collapsing.

By daring for a moment to reveal her pain, she risked her tenuous sense of security on the rare chance I might care. Taking that fleeting chance, she looked up into my face. The moment her eyes found mine, a charge of emotion arced between us like a banshee current leaping toward a grounding rod.

On being seen—*really seen*—she drew in a gasp. While holding her gaze for an instant, I watched her lower lip begin to tremble while her huge brown eyes filled with liquid glass.

Just as quickly, her gaze broke away. Apparently not knowing where to turn, she rotated back toward the horse. Staring at nothing, she continued brushing mechanically. Silent tears streaked down her flawless cheeks. Gathering together under her chin, fluid sorrow dropped without herald and vanished forever into the earth beneath us. In that moment I wondered how many other tears had fallen. How often had she held herself and cried alone in her prison of sorrow, hidden from the sight of all?

Hoping that a quiet moment would draw Angela out, I said nothing and continued brushing shoulder to shoulder with her. After several deep breaths she began to gather herself. She ran the back of her slender hand under her jaw and swept away the remaining droplets that gave witness to the depth of her grief.

It was time.

With one more heavy breath, Angela steeled herself by resting both hands on Teva's sturdy body. "I cannot live with my dad," she began, "because last year my two brothers, my grandmother, *and* my dad…were all killed."

From anyone else's viewpoint I'm sure we made an endearing sight—two friends brushing a golden mare under a late afternoon sun. Yet the moment was anything but endearing.

I felt as if I'd just been crushed by a wrecking ball! My first recognizable thought was a stammering, *Lord…I don't know what to say!* My throat tightened. *Lord…I don't know how to comfort her.*

Rising from the stillness that enveloped us, a small voice rang in my heart like a bell on a cold day. Though spoken with softness, its proven authority reverberated within my chest. *Yes, child, you do! Your words of comfort will be as natural as your own breath. You have not only felt this comfort; you have lived it. Tell her of the healing that I have accomplished in your life. Tell her what I have done for you.*

My gaze rested on the distant horizon. Beset by an unexpected whirlwind of memories, I was carried back to my childhood. Suddenly *I* was the little raven-haired girl struggling to survive a murderous attack of sorrow, confusion, and hopelessness. Looking down as if from an angel's view, I saw through the fallow tree branches a child writhing in the tilled soil below. Her small hands desperately clenched fistfuls of dirt in an effort to hold on to the hands of the beloved parents she'd lost. Facedown, she sobbed, screamed, coughed, and wretched. Wailing the name of the only One who could save her, she cried, "Jesus, Jesus, help me!"

With that simple plea the Lord of All descended through time and space and knelt beside a breaking child. Once I was just like the waif who stood shivering beside me, a devastated child dying of a broken heart.

I faced Teva and obeyed my God by simply speaking and trusting Him to provide the words. "Oh, Angela, I'm sorry. So sorry. But, baby girl, I'm moved that you came to the ranch today...and I'm especially glad that you're with me. Out of all those who are here today, I'm quite certain I'm the only one who can honestly say I know how you feel. And you know something, girl? I can tell you from experience that you're going to be okay. I know that it doesn't seem like it right now...but you're going to make it through this."

I turned and looked directly into Angela's eyes. "Wanna hear how I know?"

If a look could be an action, her eyes were on their knees, pleading for an answer.

"On the day that *my* parents died, I was so devastated I didn't think I could live another minute. And in my grief I cried out to Jesus for help. What I now know is the Lord of All took the little hand that was reaching out to Him...and He's *never* let go. Not then, not now, not ever. Since I asked Jesus to help me, He's never stopped helping me. Even though there were times when I felt alone, *I never was*...because from that day He's never left me."

I held Angela's gaze and allowed a knowing smile to slowly cross my lips. In my memory our places were again reversed. Now I was the desperate child looking up into the wrinkled, kind face of my grandmother. Suddenly I was following her, carrying a basket of wet laundry to the clothesline. With practiced care she hung each soggy item to dry in the backyard. Looking down at me, she said with conviction, "We're going to make it through this. You'll see." Perhaps because of the way she said it, I believed her. I didn't realize I was crying until she gently took the basket out of my arms, laid it aside, and scooped me into a hug. Grandmother and granddaughter wept together as damp laundry wafted around us in the warm breeze.

Though grieving herself over the loss of her daughter, my grandmother never lost sight of what she could do to help. She knew we had already lost enough. Without flinching, she and my grandfather chose to keep my two older sisters and me together as a family.

My grandma was the vibrant life ring that Jesus tossed out to save three little girls. Beth Everest, known to me and my sisters as "Mimi," was five feet of concrete poured into selfless, loving hands and feet. In a time of great sorrow, she looked beyond her own grief and wounding and saw the wounded. Her focus didn't reside on herself but on what she could do. And what Jesus did through her saved my life.

During many a summer's twilight, we sat together on the cement steps that led into our home. With a bucket of peas between us, we'd shell them into large bowls that we had balanced between our knees. This was our special time to talk. Sometimes while shelling we counted the bats that flew out of a magnificent oak tree in the front pasture. Sometimes we laughed at the giant toads that dined on the bugs that fell from an old light bulb by the front door. Sometimes Mimi talked late into the evening, telling me stories of how she loved my grandfather, how she loved my mom, and how she loved me. In my vast desert of despair, her unfailing love was my oasis of hope.

Mimi was not perfect, but she was my hero. She realized how deeply this child loved horses. In one bold decision she bought a small horse for me. My life was never the same after that. What I've since learned is that a good horse will intuitively take you where you often cannot go on your own—yet where you most need to go.

It was on the back of a small horse with crooked front legs that I felt safe, that I felt loved, and that I fell in love with Jesus. Firefly, my little roan mare, became the refuge where my broken heart discovered the healing redemption of my Lord—all because a grandmother purchased a horse for her granddaughter. The impact of this single choice rings through my life to this day. *This day...*

Angela's eyes were riveted to mine, her lips slightly parted, silently imploring me to continue.

"What should have destroyed me," I said, "Jesus turned around, and with His love He gave me life...and not just me... Look around you. Look at all the kids in this place." Her eyes drifted momentarily, then locked back on mine.

"In His timing Jesus is the only One who can transform our pain into something amazing, something beautiful," I said. "He is the only One who can take our jagged scars and transform them into beauty marks for His glory. Pain can either destroy or define. Angela, we don't have to be destroyed by our pain. In Jesus' hands how we grow *through* our pain can define us. In time the healing from our own brokenness can be so powerful, so complete, that we can actually help lead the way for others to know the same healing from God that has been extended to us. Baby, if Jesus can do this for me, He can do it for you too."

For the rest of the afternoon, Angela's words flowed like a river bursting through an earthen dam. With laughter and tears we spoke freely of life and death and much in between. When it was time for her to go, I hugged her tight and kissed both of her cheeks. Angela thanked me for everything. With shining eyes she exclaimed that because of our conversation, she had some new ideas she was really excited about.

As this tiny girl walked down the driveway, I thought again of my grandmother, so similar in stature. Mimi may have been small, but her determination to fight for me and my future was immeasurably huge. She gave me hope, a reason to live when I needed it most. I prayed that Jesus would find someone to do the same for the young woman I'd just met.

Near the bottom of the driveway, Angela turned to look back at me one more time. Her beautiful brown face spread into a glorious smile.

My heart warmed as I smiled back. *Maybe,* I thought, *He already has.*

Warriors of Hope

> A true warrior understands that every pain
> and scar—when placed in the hands of the
> King—has great purpose. The Lord calls us
> to grow *through* our suffering and fight for
> those without hope.

It's an amazing truth that out of our King's great mercy, He delivers us through our suffering so that our past hurts can heal others' futures.

Everyone will know suffering. When we're crushed by pain, if we cry out to Jesus, He comforts us. He offers His healing compassion in such abundance that we can actually *give* His comfort to those around us who are going through similar hardships. Every instance of pain we experience in this life is an opportunity to grow a deeper reliance on God's peace, comfort, and strength. Every moment of suffering can make us grow stronger. Every time we walk *through* our pain, it deepens the confidence we have in our King to deliver us through *any* circumstance for our growth and His glory.

A wise friend once shared guidelines she considers when faced with a difficult or painful challenge:

- Does God know about it? (Yes. He's God.)
- If God knows about it, has He allowed it? (Yes. He's God.)
- If God knows about it and has allowed it in my life, how does He wish for me to grow through it? (Fill in the answer.)
- If God knows about it and has allowed it in my life because I need to grow in this specific area, am I going to trust my King—whether I understand this painful circumstance or not—and obediently step forward in faith, knowing that His best plan is to give me a "future and a hope" (Jeremiah 29:11)?

Our King loves us so much. He gives each of us His mantle of grace when we go through difficult times. It is His great design that through our difficult seasons, we will see Him as He truly is—the One who supplies our every need, the One who holds us up by His righteous right hand, the One who suffered death so we would know His life—and be able to share that life with those who are hurting.

When I was lost and felt wounded beyond repair, the Lord used my grandmother to give me refuge and a new beginning. When everything was taken from me, she provided a home, family, love, and encouragement. Any influence I've had on the lives of others through the ranch, my testimony, and my relationships would not have been possible without my Mimi. When I had none, she gave me hope.

Many years later I had the privilege of helping to return the favor. I had already received Christ on the day I took my grandmother by the hand and led her down the long aisle to the front of our church. It was there, together, that we knelt and prayed for her to receive the saving grace of Jesus Christ. Because she led me to hope, I was able to lead her to the Author of hope.

Scripture says, "In his kindness God called you to his eternal glory by means of Jesus Christ. After you have suffered a little while, he will restore, support, and strengthen you, and he will place you on a firm foundation" (1 Peter 5:10).

When we choose to answer the call of our Lord, we become like a bow in His hands. A bow is useful only when it's drawn. It's the drawing, the ability to handle tension, that gives a bow its value. With a little draw, there is little release. Yet each time we submit to God, we expand our trust and faith and grow more flexible, resilient, and strong. Over time we are able to flex into a full draw and know His full release. The bigger the draw, the farther our arrows fly for Him. The farther they fly, the greater the impact we make on the hearts of those around us who need help.

Trust yourself to your King. Rest in knowing your every scar is purposed for His glory. Choose to become a bow in His hands. You'll discover that as you fight for His hope and truth, He will *never* fail you.

17

THE RACE

Don't You *Ever* Quit!

Many years of ski racing had brought me to an exciting pinnacle: I had qualified to compete in the U.S. Olympic Biathlon Team Trials. This unlikely combination of cross-country skate skiing and rifle marksmanship began in Scandinavia. Originating as a practical method of hunting off skis, biathlon also doubled as an effective method of border patrol. Today it's a challenging sport that blends two contrasting skills.

The Olympic trials for biathlon were to be held in Anchorage, Alaska. I was excited about spending some time in this powerful place. Graced with the financial help of several benevolent friends, I was on my way. During my flight I marveled at the vast sea of powdery white mountains below me. Each shouldered the soft, pinkish lavender mantle of winter twilight. During this peaceful interlude, I had time to reflect on my personal journey and the magnificent chain of events that had brought me to this rare finale.

Unlike the other women I'd be racing with, I would not be vying for a berth on the Olympic team. I was realistic about the fact that I was neither skilled nor experienced enough to compete for our country. But I *had* qualified to race at this level several years before and wasn't able to fulfill this dream because I couldn't afford it. Having qualified a second time, I didn't wish to let the opportunity pass by again.

Of the twenty-nine women who qualified, I would be one of the few competing in these trials who did not race on a sponsored team, have a coach, or receive subsidized gear or free ski endorsements. I came alone. I would also be, to my knowledge, one of the few women who was not a full-time, elite athlete. Instead, I worked many different jobs to pay for the sport I loved. Several years of regret over missing the trials the first time was enough for me. I'd earned the right to race at this level. That's all I truly wanted—a chance to try.

Though I had trained hard for this event, the other women had trained much harder for much longer. For them, a great deal was on the line. Years of focused preparation hung in the balance. Each hoped to compete in the Olympics. Because of this, I was aware my nearly random presence might not be welcomed by this tight-knit group even though I knew everyone I'd be racing with.

Upon arriving at the quarters where all the competitors were staying, I looked for any familiar faces that might be able to answer a few questions. I needed to know where the biathletes were staging, if there was transportation to the course, and where the waxing rooms were.

It wasn't long before I spotted two women I knew. In my excitement I embraced one and stepped toward the other. She abruptly straight-armed me in the chest and snapped, "Don't *touch* me. I don't *do* hugs." I stood back in stunned silence. A smattering of inconsequential words fell between us before they blithely walked away.

So this is how it's going to be.

After training on the course for nearly a month while living among the bristle of these territorial women, I welcomed the first race in the series. Slated to be a fifteen-kilometer individual race, it would encompass five skiing loops and four shooting stages, one between each loop. The shooting position for each stage would alternate between prone and standing. With only five bullets to hit five targets, every missed shot would add an additional minute of penalty to the racer's overall time. With competitors finishing within seconds of one another, the addition of a single minute weighed as heavy as an entire day.

I had trained for years, I had saved the money, I had gotten the time off work, and I had sacrificed—all for this day. Today was my turn to race in the U.S. Olympic trials.

Excited, I reached the course very early. My prerace habit drove me first to check the start list to see where I'd be in the lineup. I scanned the sheet and felt a faint clench in my chest. I scanned it again...and again.

My name was nowhere to be found.

After a flurry of questions, I finally located the race director and pointed out the error. He acknowledged my revelation with a slight "Huh," shrugging it off by saying they must have lost my packet of race applications. To my massive relief he concluded, "Since this start list has already been sanctioned, we cannot change it. The only way you can race is if we tack you on last behind all the other women." Although this wasn't a desired position, I was grateful to be penciled in and have a chance to race.

Relieved, I skied out to the firing range and began the process of zeroing my rifle. This vital procedure recalibrates a rifle to the greatest degree of accuracy for the present conditions. As expected, the staging area was a complete crush of coaches, equipment, and athletes. Trainers and sponsors hauled out mind-boggling amounts of gear. One area looked like a neon picket fence with what appeared to be dozens of new skis strategically placed side by side for participants who had earned them.

Unlike these women whose sponsors granted them armloads of new skis, boots, poles, and racing attire every season, I would be racing with the same three pairs of skis I'd owned since the start of my career. These skis were priceless to me. Not only were they all I had, but they had been given to me by a dear friend, along with a single pair of perfect graphite poles.

Year after year I'd raced with this same gear. Each piece was a trusted companion. We'd experienced and accomplished so much together. My upper body was a perfect fit to transfer power through this lone pair of poles. My lower body intimately knew the design, balance, and feel of each ski. My skis even bore a handwritten set of initials, a private message

I'd inscribed on the tips to encourage my heart forward when the pain was great. This was not simply my gear. It was a part of me.

Because zeroing is achieved in a prone position, I protected my poles by stowing them in an upright stance along the low fence behind the range. Since I was alone, I was forced to shoot five shots, get up, ski back to a general spotting scope, track where my shots had gone, evaluate the needed clicks to bring the group into zero, make the adjustment, and ski back to the firing line. I repeated this process many times until all shots were within a nickel-size area in the center of the target.

In the crush of athletes and their entourage, a coach began to set up for his team right behind me. I rose to my feet and started to ski back to the fence to reload my clips. As if watching a slow-motion collision and being helpless to stop it, I saw one of his heavy spotting scopes topple over. It landed with a sickening *crunch* directly on my poles!

For others this would've been a minor inconvenience, but for me it was catastrophic. I'd just witnessed my only pair of poles—*my friends*—destroyed right in front of me.

Mouth agape in disbelief, I skied up and pointed out to the coach what he had inadvertently just done. He simply stared at me, then at my poles, and declared they weren't broken. I picked them up, placed them firmly in my hands, and made the same quick downward thrust that one would make at the start of a race. My right pole exploded as if an umbrella had opened inside its narrow shaft.

He dismissed me with a palms-up shrug that a person might give to someone who owns a garage full of extra poles. I explained that these were my *only* poles. His expression clearly showed he didn't believe me.

The best the coach could manage was to offer me *one* of his personal poles out of the hundreds that perforated the staging area. It was eight inches longer than my remaining pole. The difference in length meant only one thing for me—pain, and lots of it. I had trained my entire racing career with the same length of pole. I knew raising my right hand eight inches higher than normal with every stride during a nine-mile race was going to create the mother of all backaches. Pushing down my rising angst, I purposed to receive his spare pole without anger and not let this distract me from doing my best.

I returned to the firing line to continue my zeroing process. After shooting several more rounds, the straight-pull bolt action on my rifle felt…different. I bolted it again and watched—to my horror—a tiny piece inexplicably fly off into the snow. I lunged to the spot where I saw it fall and was able to quickly retrieve the miniscule part. Immediately I scooped up all my things and rushed to the indoor staging area.

En route, a train wreck of scenarios collided in my mind. In all my years of shooting, totaling tens of thousands of shots, this had *never* happened. In the world of biathlon rifles, mine was one of the simplest, with few and heavy moving parts. The Soviet Baikal Vostok was renowned for remarkable durability in less-than-ideal circumstances. This was not a fastidious, prima-donna rifle. Mine was the less prestigious, less expensive, and often-maligned workhorse of the biathlon world. At that time there were only four other known rifles like mine in all the United States. With the race starting soon, I knew that if I couldn't get this rifle back together quickly, no one would.

After bursting into the staging area, I spread out my gear and rapidly dismantled my rifle. As if I were in a timed military-ops training drill, I then reassembled it as fast as I could. As another biathlete passed by, I asked if her coach might have any experience with this rifle. Her over-the-shoulder response was, "That's what you get for buying a Soviet rifle."

Although a verbal rather than a physical slap, I still felt its fiery sting across my face. Again I was reminded of how alone I truly was.

Once my rifle assembly was complete, I gingerly tested the bolting action. Everything felt normal. I rebolted over and over, harder and faster each time. When it showed no sign of its prior mysterious trouble, I thanked the Lord for His intervention, gathered my gear, and skied as hard as I could back out to the range. As I slid up to the entrance, I saw a course official taping it off, formally signaling that the range was *closed*!

My rifle was completely unzeroed. Since the prone target is about the size of a silver dollar, I would probably miss all my prone shots. Out of twenty shots, fully half would likely be lost; ten minutes would be added to my time. *Ten minutes!* Before my race even started, I was already days behind.

My heart fell like a stone. After all this work I wanted to cry.

Willing myself to stay focused, I sought out the man who had broken my pole and pleaded with him to help me. I asked him to watch me ski into the range once the race had started, spot my first group, and advise me how to click for the next three trips into the range. This is what all coaches do for their teams, and since he had severely hindered my chances of doing well, it seemed like an appropriate request. My presence at this race series threatened few, certainly none of his skiers. For me, this was only about the opportunity to compete in the U.S. Olympic trials.

Beginning my warm-up process, I took note of the weather and course conditions. Although twenty degrees is not considered that cold, the humidity combined with a brisk wind made it feel closer to zero. The ambient weather had been even less kind. Several days earlier, falling snow had turned into falling rain. Once the storm front passed, the rain-sodden snow had frozen into a solid, bricklike consistency, making the course extremely fast and sketchy.

Now it looked as if a new storm was approaching. A heavy, ominous overcast filled the Alaskan sky. The flat, shadowless day was perfect for a shooter but, since it camouflaged all terrain, horrible for a skier.

Every biathlete has an individual and very specific method of readying body and mind to race at optimum performance. This process entails a series of skiing slower laps to gradually warm the body. As the muscles begin to heat, hot laps at near maximum speed are added to the mix to prepare the heart and lungs for premium output. This process is done with great calculation and timing so that once the athlete is warmed up, she will immediately begin the countdown toward ignition before her body begins to cool down. At this point, timing is imperative, because once the warm-up suit comes off, the competitor has a relatively small window before she begins to cool down, tighten up, and use vital stores of glycogen. The colder the conditions, the smaller the time window the racer has to get her warmups off and ski race started.

The lady biathletes were under way. Like brilliant-colored rockets, every thirty seconds a woman exploded from the start gate in an impressive flurry of power and grace. "Three...two...one...go! Good luck, racer," the start official repeated in a serious monotone to every skier.

I was only slightly aware that it was bitterly cold once I had peeled down to nothing more than my Lycra racing suit. Completely adrenalized, I skied into the start box and assumed an aggressive start position. The official began his countdown: "Ten...nine...eight..."

My body felt like a volatile coil compressed into a launch position. "Seven...six..."

With my eyes straight ahead, I felt an instinctive deepening in my knees and hips. I was a lioness ready to leap into the hunt.

"Five...four... Hey, wait a minute. Who *are* you?"

Frantic about completing my countdown, I gushed the entire story of my allegedly lost application and official add-on in one second flat. The official blinked several times as he studied his list. Suddenly his mouth pressed into a straight line. Then he exhaled forcefully. "Well, no one told *me*!" he said, grinding the words between his teeth. "You can't start now. It will throw off the entire men's list. You'll have to go after all the men. No, wait, we have a couple dozen junior racers after them. You'll have to go completely last."

I was astonished. I couldn't believe what I was hearing!

Stunned, I stepped out of the start box and back into the bull pen. In bewildered silence I pulled on my warmups as male racers crowded into the small arena. Because the course was now filled with competitors, there was nowhere for me to warm up except a tiny circle outside the starting area.

Repeatedly I felt anxiety climb into my throat and squeeze. I knew that a breakdown would be the end of my day. I fought the crush in my chest by willing myself to focus on skiing circles so absurdly small that the length of my skis hardly fit within them.

While circling I had plenty of time to consider my physiology education. I knew that the human musculature and liver can store only a finite amount of glycogen. This is the quick-burning "gasoline" that fuels the body in both aerobic and anaerobic activity. Once this fuel source is depleted, the body must resort to other, less efficient means of energy production. Because I didn't know how many men or junior racers there were, I couldn't leave my circling post to go indoors and warm up. My weakening heart, muscles, and hope all consumed vital energy. Soon all I felt was intense cold.

I continued to circle…for nearly two hours.

Completely exhausted and rigid with cold, I was at last allowed back into the bull pen to make final preparations to begin my race. The start official looked surprised to see me as I slid back into the box and onto the line. "Three…two…one…go! Good luck, racer," I heard him mutter as I sprinted away. Having to use part of the first loop to warm up again, I felt terrible.

Skiing as fast as I was able, I skated into the range and popped off five quick shots. As expected, they were all misses. While jumping back up to my skis and heading out of the range, I looked into the gallery at the coach who'd promised to spot for me. He was talking to a friend and hadn't even noticed I'd come in. I called his name, and he turned and glowered at me. He'd clearly not only forgotten our agreement, but he was also annoyed that I'd interrupted him.

Again I fought the rise of complete despair. I skated hard out of the range.

In my beleaguered effort to make up time, I powered down the trail like a human freight train. In this particular race the second loop was the longest. As I sprinted into a major intersection, only then did I realize that all the course officials were *gone*. They must have thought the race was over; there was no one to guide me in the correct direction. Although the loops were designated by color, they were not marked in any manner I could distinguish.

Instantly I chose the course that had the most wear. Because it showed the most ski tracks, I felt certain this was the right direction. As I ventured into the forest, a slow dawning began to rise in my frantic brain. The skate tracks had thinned out. Everyone had turned around.

I was hammering down nothing more than a warm-up loop. I was completely off course!

Turning around and retracing the useless distance, I went back to the unmanned intersection and scoured the area for any identification of the right trail. Seeing a flattened color marker down in the snow, I chose the course upon which it lay, hoping that when the marker was struck, it had fallen onto the correct track.

Fight for this! echoed in my head. I skated into the range for my second shooting stage. This time I stood. With my unzeroed rifle I was grateful to hit three targets. Struggling, I tried to stay positive and ski the next loop fast.

I arrived at the range for my third shooting phase, where I would be prone again. Knowing that I would certainly miss all five targets, I shot as quickly as I could and jumped up to my skis again. While moving forward, reslinging my rifle onto my back, and returning my hands to my pole grips, one of my poles slipped from under my arm. The tip hit the snow right in front of my boot.

The result was much like ramming a broomstick into the spokes of a bicycle.

I didn't even have time to put my hands out before landing *hard* on my chin. As if cracking my head on an icy surface wasn't bad enough, this sad chain reaction unfolded right in front of the spectators' grandstand. And if that didn't kill every last molecule of pride within me, scrambling up off the snow and having a camera—an ESPN camera—pushed into my face did.

The only documentation my family would have of my entire journey to get to this point would be of my missing all my shots and then tripping myself in front of God and country on national television. And if one person on earth might've missed my idiotic wreck, that individual would certainly be able to catch it on the sports comedy reel later that night!

All fragments of pride I had about racing in the Olympic trials for biathlon lay shattered beyond repair as I skated over them and out of the range.

Still driving hard, I entered a nearly empty range for the last five standing shots of the race. Again I hit three targets and dropped two. The crowds were gone now, and the entire area lay vacant and hollow. Grateful they'd left, I felt completely deflated and embarrassed that I'd fallen in such a dumb way in front of everyone.

This feeling exposed a deeper sadness. The great depth of my humiliation was only eclipsed by the greater depth of my pride. None of my vanquished efforts to do my best mattered now. What more could possibly go wrong on this day? That single thought seemed to hang in my draft as I reslung my rifle and skied away.

The last loop before the finish consisted of a steep descent that swept sharply through a maze of turns toward the icy seas of the Cook Inlet. As the snow continued to harden in the dilapidating weather, I felt as if I were howling down a bobsled course instead of a skate-skiing track.

Crouching into a full tuck, I fought to keep my chattering boards under me. Banking one ski-shuddering turn after another, my eyes watered from the combined assault of cold and speed. As I screamed around one of the final turns, I looked down the track to see a fully grown moose standing broadside across the trail!

She was huge, and because she stood perpendicular to the course, she blocked the entire track.

At the speed I was traveling, I had about two seconds to decide if I could fit under her belly or under her tail. *Belly? Tail? Belly? TAIL!*

Like a rocket, I flashed behind her. She lunged forward and kicked straight out at the sudden intruder beneath her hocks.

Thankfully, she missed. My speed carried me well beyond her re-flexes. My prayer was reduced to, *Don't fall, don't fall, don't fall!* During a brief backward glance, I saw her spin toward me and take several trotting strides down the course. Her large ears were pressed back, and her head was down in a position of clear warning: "If I could catch you, I would *kill* you!"

By God's mercy I didn't fall. The icy track quickly carried me beyond her threat.

It wasn't until I reached the bottom of the incline and began racing across the flats that I realized this was the highest heart rate I'd ever expe-rienced while skiing *down* a hill! Now the only obstacle that stood between me and the finish line was one of the toughest uphills in the entire park. The incline was known by a number of foul names because it was so difficult to climb with a body already taxed to its limits.

I rounded the base of the slope. As expected, the difference in my poles was exacting a brutal toll. I felt as if a burning knife had been plunged between my shoulder blades. Every stride, accompanied by rais-ing my arms over my head and driving my poles into the ice, fanned the searing heat up my neck and through the back of my skull.

Whether it was the compounded traumas of the day or seeing the hoofs of an incensed moose flash past my head, once I started up the flank of the rising slope, my entire body felt as if it were being consumed by an internal inferno. Because the first pitch of the hill did not deviate left or right but rose straight up, my heart rate soared with it.

Never in my life had I felt a lactic-acid buildup cause a more agoniz-ing muscle burn. The pain was so intense I was certain that any minute my quadriceps would combust into flames! With a fleeting glimpse I looked down to see if my Lycra was melting off. Instead, I saw something just as troubling on my right thigh—*blood*.

A quick swipe of my gloved fist under my nose revealed the source. Apparently the strain of the day had taken a greater toll than I'd realized. Vessels in my nose had burst under the tension and were streaming bright-red blood down my face. Having never suffered a spontaneous nosebleed in my life, I was left to wonder—again—*Why, of all days, would it be today?*

Worn down by the smorgasbord of difficulties, negative thoughts began to hammer my heart like a battering ram. Together they worked to crush my resolve. *Lord, what am I doing here? Why am I even still trying? After working for so long, I never thought it would turn out like* this.

My race was an absolute disaster. I'm exhausted and traumatized. I feel broken and alone… My strength is gone… My hope is gone… There's nothing redeeming about any of this… Who on earth really cares? Nothing that I've done even matters, none of it. I should just quit!

From this private incinerator of agony and under full emotional attack, I glanced up the hill. Startled by a movement, I quickly looked up again. I was surprised to see a heavily bundled figure standing alone. This person was perched approximately one hundred yards above me, near the course. Because all the other race officials had left—including the moose sweepers—I was perplexed about this one resolute soul who remained.

It was a woman. She was dressed in a large, light-colored snowmobile suit. She held a clipboard in her heavily gloved hands and was apparently the last of those who kept a tally, making sure that every racer skied every loop. Standing like a sentry on a small shelf that had been kicked into the side of the hill, she looked down on me with an unwavering gaze.

I can only imagine what she must have thought as she watched me lurch up one of the most grueling hills in the park, breathing like a steam engine and smeared with blood. What a pitiful image of a biathlete, one who was most certainly lost, certainly alone, certainly struggling to make it.

In accordance with the events of the day, I waited for her to say something obvious such as, "Girl, you look like death on a cracker!" Or, more in keeping with the attitude of others, I expected she would ignore me altogether.

She did neither.

Among all her choices to malign and despise, she chose none. Nor did she look away. Instead, the solitary woman watched me intently.

As I closed the distance between us, a final thought fell to the floor of my soul: *Lord, on this day I don't think I can bear any more.*

When I was a dozen yards away, the woman looked down at her clipboard, presumably to write my bib number on her list. Looking back up, she fixed her eyes on mine and muttered, "Good job, number seventy-seven."

Surprised, I stared at her, not really sure if I'd heard her right. In my haggard state I wasn't certain she was really talking to me…encouraging me?

Our eyes locked.

Again she spoke in a serious tone. "C'mon, girl, you can do it. Get up this hill." It took a moment for me to realize that she was…*cheering*… for *me*.

Unable to speak, I flashed a bloody smile. She smiled back. "C'mon, seventy-seven! Fight! *Fight!*" I watched in amazement as she bit off one glove and then the other. Sacrificing her own comfort in the bitter cold, she began to clap her bare hands so I could hear them. "Go, seventy-seven. Go! *C'mon!*"

Fueled by her encouragement, I skied past her and winked. Clapping as hard as she could, she continued to cheer for me as I climbed up and away and into the forest above. Far below I could hear her voice ringing through the trees: "Gooooo, girl! Gooooo! *Don't you ever quit!*"

As if spoken by an angel, her voice echoes in my heart to this day. Because on that day, I know I heard the voice of my King.

Spectators and officials had abandoned the finish line. I was the last to complete the race. I crossed the line and collapsed in the icy snow. While heaving to catch my breath, a lone race official appeared and stepped over my sprawled skis on his way to the range. He looked back over his shoulder and called, "Sorry, I thought the race was already over."

Struggling to catch my breath, I lay nearly motionless for long moments. Tears slid across my face and disappeared into the snow.

Once the fire subsided and my breath returned, I scrubbed the blood off my face with a handful of snow, pulled on my warmups, and skated back down the hill through the forest.

I wanted to thank the one and only soul who sought to encourage me.

When I reached her post, nothing remained but the small ledge upon which she'd stood. Even though I searched for her throughout the rest of the week-long race series, I never saw her again.

She will never know how the gift she gave me that day has permanently changed my life.

Never Quit

> A warrior is not distracted by the entanglements of this life. She answers God's call to fix her eyes and her energy on running hard to the end of the race...where her King awaits.

Years to ponder have given me a perspective that I've grown to love and appreciate. I can no longer think about the race in Anchorage without also considering how it perfectly captured the truth in the Bible's book of Hebrews, chapters 11 and 12. The author of Hebrews sets the stage by simply asking, "What is faith?" He then answers his own question with the reply, "It is the confident assurance that what we hope for is going to happen. It is the evidence of things we cannot yet see" (Hebrews 11:1).

Next, he paints an unforgettable picture of remarkable, beautiful, diverse individuals whose lives demonstrated true faith. By faith, men and women did extraordinary things for the love of their King. By faith, they led nations, defeated vast enemies, and walked through oceans on dry land. By faith, they shut the mouths of lions, quenched the flames of fire, and escaped death by the edge of a sword.

By faith, their weakness was turned into strength.

Also by faith others preferred to die rather than turn from God. They placed their hope in the Resurrection. Some were mocked, beaten, chained, and whipped. Some died by stoning and the sword. Some were *sawed in two*. Others were hungry, oppressed, and mistreated and lived in terrible circumstances. They were too good for this world. All these people received our King's approval because of their faith. Yet *none* of them received all that God has promised:

> For God had far better things in mind for us that would also benefit them, for they can't receive the prize at the end of the race until *we* finish the race. Therefore, since we are surrounded by such a huge crowd of witnesses to the life of faith, let us strip off every weight that slows us down, especially the sin that so easily hinders our progress. And let us *run with endurance* the race that God has set before us. We do this by keeping our eyes on Jesus, on whom our faith depends from start to finish. (Hebrews 11:40–12:2)

Friends, no matter how difficult this race of life gets and how lonely we might feel, we are not alone in our struggles.

Every believer who has ever lived is poised and watching. Just like that woman on the hill in Anchorage, they are cheering, shouting, praying, screaming, clapping, and doing "the wave" in an effort to continually encourage us—*you*—to keep going, to finish well, to *never quit*.

Like an Olympic runner carrying the torch, believers have passed truth to other believers down through the ages. Now they encourage *you* to run this flaming message of truth all the way home. They cheer as a direct reflection of the One who leads them all. Jesus Christ directs this heavenly assembly with shouts of victory, whispers of encouragements, peals of knowing laughter, and songs of comfort. He does this by constantly reassuring each of us that He—our King—is right beside us step for step, stride for stride to the very end.

As Christian women, we're not racing for ourselves but for *all* believers. Every stride we take toward our King brings us closer to completing the work of faith that all the righteous men and women before us began long ago. This magnificent picture of glory will not be complete until each of us is faithful to finish the race.

Only then will we all receive the prize. Only then will the bride of Christ be complete.

This race is so much bigger than what we see in the mirror. Every narrow-minded step toward our own desires takes us off course. Each selfish stride leads us away from those we were sent to serve, the huge crowd of witnesses who are encouraging us home, and most of all...our King.

Now is the time to stay focused on what's truly important: faithfully racing toward our God.

Like skiers on fresh snow, we all leave tracks in this life. Our every word and action marks a course for others to follow. Make no mistake, in your own unique way, you were designed to lead those around you who are staggering in exhaustion.

Because of what Christ has done for you, you are completely equipped to do much more for others than you ever thought possible: "So take a new grip with your tired hands and stand firm on your shaky legs. Mark out a straight path for your feet. Then those who follow you, though they are weak and lame, will not stumble and fall but will become strong" (Hebrews 12:12–13). Each of us is called to help lead those around us to finish this battle of faith.

Within this race of giving, leading, falling, and bleeding, each of us will know loops of deep sorrow and grief. We will all experience hills that grind us well beyond the ability to eat and sleep. These are the times when God alone is our comfort and strength.

Although we might feel too weak to fight on, we are never too weak to lean on Him.

Often it is in our seasons of greatest breakage that God's greatest strength, love, joy, and mercy are revealed. Despite my best efforts in the biathlon race, I'm certain I finished in last place, the position of greatest shame and scorn. But when we choose to relinquish our desire to compete for ourselves in exchange for a higher calling of running the race of faith for our King, *everyone* wins.

Since my difficult biathlon experience, I've learned that no matter what phase of life's race I'm in, if I quiet my thoughts and still my heart, I can hear the voice of my King calling, *Run, girl. Run! Every step of faith you take brings you closer to Me. When you cross the finish line, you will run right into My arms. Keep running, child! Don't you ever quit!*

18

THE BATTLE

For the King Alone

It was now well past midnight, and I was still working in my perch at the top of our ranch property. I was hoping to finish a time-sensitive project before morning. Reaching both fists toward the ceiling, I indulged in a long-overdue stretch.

Wanting to relax my head for a moment, I silenced the taskmaster of focused thought and allowed my mind to roam. It wasn't long before the likeness of the woman returned. Before, her image had seemed diffused, her form softly shifting. But now she appeared with living sharpness and clarity.

She's free. She is standing right before me, *with me*.

Looking up, she blinks her eyes in astonishment, as if seeing for the very first time. Her gaudy clothing was burned away when she chose the sword of righteousness. Now she wears a simple tunic, boots, and a sturdy leather belt accompanied by leather cuffs and greaves. Her hair gleams with a glory beyond color. Her chest is covered by a breastplate of unearthly metal. Although it is steely in appearance, dazzling light passes through it, the same radiance still emanating from the center of her body and illuminating the area around her.

With the long sword clutched in her right hand, the new warrior inhales deeply, breathing in the very light that streams from her chest.

While doing so, her eyes began to shine as never before, filling with the truth of her King.

Voices of furious and frightened wickedness hiss all around her: "She's *awake*! Run!" "Her real eyes are open! Find reinforcements!" "She's just made the decision to start doing what she's learned from the Book. She's tapped into the Source. Get help now!" "This one's fully committed... She's gonna be dangerous!"

Her thoughts are now so strong they can be seen in her actions. Swinging her sword in wide arcs, the warrior feels its balance, its eternal power. She understands the purpose of this weapon: to herald hope, fight for the weak, and cut a path through the blackness for the love of God to flow. This blade is the very *Word* of her King, and it is a part of her now.

Awareness is building within her. Slowly she realizes that what she does under pressure defines what she truly believes. Her focus lifts, moving beyond the things, the distractions of this world. Now she looks directly at her foes and actually sees them. She recognizes her enemies for what they truly are. With a new and unwavering authority, she points her sword at the shadowy figures that surround her and commands, "No one can serve two masters. Leave...*now*!"

A voice, dripping with evil, responds, "I don't think so, *princess*!"

Once fearful, she is now fearless. She raises her blade and steps toward her black adversaries. "I'm taking back this ground," she growls through clenched teeth, "in the name of Jesus Christ!"

The filthy smirking of her enemies is cut off the instant they hear the Name. As if the mere sound of it burns, they scream and cower, covering their ears as they back away.

The warrior takes a step forward, then another. Each stride repels the armies of darkness. Every well-placed blow of her sword only makes it sharper. Soon she's cut a path to the front lines and is fighting shoulder to shoulder with other warriors of the Living God.

The air fills with the foul stench of rancid wickedness. Flames rise before her but give no light. They burn but do not destroy. What was sent to incinerate her instead tempers and strengthens her. She senses the great enemies of demonic blackness rushing in to destroy her. She engages them, swords clashing and sparking with each strike. Though she can't see them, the warrior realizes other soldiers of light are close by. She also knows she must defend the territory the King has entrusted only to her.

Through the darkness she shouts to the others, "The swarms of darkness can have no more... *Hold the line!*"

She hears the deafening clatter of countless swords engaged in a struggle for life and death. The breastplate of her King's light, love, and life illuminates the dim theater around her. She fights with everything she has: heart, soul, mind, and strength.

Suddenly steel flashes on her left. She feels intense pain in her side. The warrior acknowledges the wound, but knowing her King was once wounded for her, she does not shrink back. She presses in and continues to fight.

Her sword moves in blurring arcs of light. Hiding in the shadows, her enemies are everywhere. The surrounding gloom is filled with arrows, clubs, stones, and fists, all trying to kill her.

Yet she does not retreat.

The warrior comprehends that no matter how much blood she sheds, no matter if she is on the verge of losing her mortal life, she will keep fighting as long as she has breath. She stands firm, knowing how this war will end! Swinging and slashing, ducking and dodging, striking, kicking, choking, clawing, she will not quit—*ever.*

The slithering hordes of darkness close in. The black horizon moves with their infinite number. The warrior is weary and wounded, yet she continues to fight the evil plague that seeks to engulf all mankind. She slashes through more couriers of pride, fear, immorality, injustice, disease, famine, and lies. Blood from a gash on her forehead mixes with sweat and flows into her eyes. She strains to see through the burning red haze.

She takes another step forward. From out of the blackness, a club smashes against her temple. Stunned by the strike, she stumbles and falls to one knee. Blood surges down her breastplate, flowing over her irrepressible light of hope. The wicked swarm descends upon her, pummeling the fallen warrior with their fists. Struggling to stand, she pushes up beneath their staggering numbers. She strains with all her might but falls back to the shadowy earth.

As her knees hit the cold, sucking mire, a thunderous *boom* splits the air.

The distant horizon flashes in a horizontal bolt of electric light. Suddenly the clash of armor and blades ceases. All becomes silent.

Every eye turns toward the growing radiance. Burning away the darkness, stabs of intense light rise like glorious arrows straight into the sky. Shimmering like luminous rivers, they swallow up the gloom.

Pure light is approaching… *It's the glory of her King!*

In the remaining blackness, screams of shock and horrified curses spew from the lips of cringing demons. Wicked, clawed hands lose their grip and start to withdraw in terror. A downpour of enemy weapons falls like an evil, metallic rain. The demonic army retreats in a panicked stampede. The morbid air fills with the putrid gasps of demons trying to flee the radiant justice of the Lamb of God. Gathering fearful momentum, they clamber and trample over one another in their desperate attempt to escape.

Suddenly the blackness shudders, then explodes like a mirror. In a brilliant display of pure annihilation, the fragments appear as sizzling missiles that burn up as they fly. Behind the warrior, a roaring wave of evil rolls away like a vicious tsunami. The hordes of the enemy scatter before a righteous flood. Burning like wicked meteors, they leave behind a million black, crisscrossing vapor trails as they incinerate into nothingness.

In an instant all darkness is completely consumed.

But this is not the great end. It is the Great Beginning.

The mighty One is approaching.

He is clothed in glorious light. His brilliance becomes the very air surrounding the warrior. No longer struggling to stand, she now collapses, kneeling low before her King. He has come—the King of kings—to ransom the redeemed.

His presence completely surrounds her and fills her. At last the warrior silently lays down her sword. Fearing even to look upon His great majesty, she keeps her head down. She knows she is battered and bleeding, still smeared with the filth she's fought against. She is not worthy to be in the presence of pure holiness.

In a voice more beautiful than any sound she's ever encountered, she hears her King say, "Arise, My love. It is time."

Still hesitant to look upon His glory, she keeps her chin tucked into her grimy chest. Slowly staggering to her feet, she feels a gentle breeze moving about her. She recognizes its presence—it is the breath of God. With her head still down, she watches in utter amazement as her wounds spontaneously heal. The bloody filth that once covered her transforms into a gown of pure light.

Still staring straight down, she senses it before she actually sees it. There, before her downcast eyes, emerges His outstretched hand.

The King of kings is reaching...*for her.*

In complete awe she gradually places her hand in His. Though she has never seen it with her eyes, His hand feels remarkably familiar. It is the identical grip of...her sword. In wondrous recognition she slowly looks up into His face.

He smiles.

The pure brilliance radiating from His countenance moves over her like a living flame of radiant love. Every moment of her mortal sorrow, suffering, and pain instantly catches fire and burns away in the presence of His all-consuming peace.

"I have always been with you, My love," He says. "And you have always been with Me."

Suddenly she understands. She *had* to choose to become a warrior because her King is a warrior. He too walked through fires—the inferno of hell itself—for all...for her. He also fought the greatest war...and won. He defeated the enemy and death itself so she could now live—forever—with Him.

If she is ever to become His perfect bride, she needs first to become His perfect reflection. This means following Him in all that He does, reflecting to the world everything that He was—and is. She needs to *choose* to love Him and then allow her love for her God to be revealed through her every thought and deed.

"Come, My bride," He says while gently turning her around. Appearing in His hand is a simple gold ring. "Receive this," He says, "as an eternal symbol of My love." Instead of placing the band on her finger, He breathes on it. Slowly the ring expands until it becomes the perfect size to fit her head. He carefully places the unadorned crown upon her brow. Smiling, He softly says, "Real beauty needs no adornments. It is your genuine love for Me that makes you radiant."

Still holding the crown on each side of her head and looking deeply into her eyes, the King speaks:

"My bride, you have fought a good fight. You have finished the race, and you have remained faithful. And now this prize awaits you—the crown of righteousness that I, the King of kings, the righteous Judge, give you on this great day. And this prize is not just for you but for *all* who eagerly look forward to My glorious return."

Once a princess, the woman has chosen to transform into a warrior so she can become the everlasting bride of Christ. Now she kneels in adoration—no longer praising her own likeness but in pure worship before the One who saved her.

Bowing low, she whispers, "For the King alone."

THE CALL

Your Turn

Be on guard. Stand true to what you believe.
Be courageous. Be strong. And everything
you do must be done with love.

—1 Corinthians 16:13–14

Dear one, it's time to rise to your feet. It's time to do your part, to carry the flame of hope, to run your race. The great calling of your God is beckoning. The vast assembly of witnesses are cheering, and the enemy will soon be attacking. But no matter what blows he might deal, and though you are wounded and worn, stand and fight in the truth that you're invincible...until the day your mighty King calls you home.

So, my friend, run *hard*—until you run into His arms.

STILL STANDING...

Recently I saw a heartwarming movie based on a true story. During the credits at the end, photographs of the actual people were streamed across the screen. After falling in love with the characters, I was deeply moved to see their real faces and read a small update about where they are now.

I thought you might appreciate the same.

"Dedication to Jenni Reiling"—True to her indomitable joy, in the last moments of her life, Jenni still chose to encourage those around her. Gripped within the final throes of cancer, she hadn't spoken, opened her eyes, or responded to anyone in days. When I walked into her room, she lay curled on her side with her right hand softly bent under her chin. I had the privilege of holding her left hand to my cheek one last time.

I leaned in close, only inches from her beautiful face, and whispered a private conversation I'd just had with her oldest son—a message of love and hope that Jenni had wished me to share with him in her stead. Through tears, I told my dying friend that her son had received her message well and would be blessed for a lifetime by this precious gift.

Photo by Boomer Reiff

Her eyes remained shut as the fingers nestled below her chin began to move. The tip of her index finger gently touched the tip of her thumb. Her remaining three fingers slowly rose, and the corners of her mouth twitched upward.

The universal gesture that everything is all right—*even in death*—became her final gift to me. Jenni was correct; because of Jesus...everything *will* be all right.

Mount Rainier

"The Fracture"—Since my near-fatal day on Mount Shasta, I've chosen to allow the lessons I learned to take root in my life. Because of this desire, I've gone on to climb and summit Mount Rainier and returned to summit my beloved friend six more times...the *right* way.

"The Wound"—Dakota continues to live the life of a much-loved and very active dog. During the writing of this book, she was frightened by a

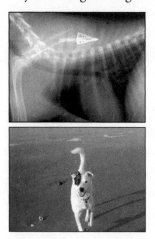

stranger, ran in front of a car traveling at highway speed, and was hit. Again her life has become the means for a miracle. Although badly wounded, she is making a slow and steady recovery. In the midst of her healing process, she remains a sweet and bright spirit for those around her and all who visit the ranch.

Kelsie and Laurie still work with me at Crystal Peaks, and both now serve as directors at the ranch. Each is a beloved friend.

"The Attack"—Since our incredible, horrifying, and hilarious encounter with the charging mother grizzly bear, I've encountered several other grizzlies without incident. As much as their power and grace intrigue me, it remains their terrifying ferocity that drives me to guard against sin in my life with the same tenacity.

By the way, the following day as we were headed home, we *did* see a moose.

"The Boulder"—Though the boulder that I regarded with such fondness is no longer on the summit of South Sister, I'm grateful to have discovered another place to sit. Not only is my new friend located in a perfect place to launch cherry pits, but it is also much farther from the edge.

"The Wilderness"—Hero lives at Crystal Peaks Youth Ranch to this day and continues to be an amazing ambassador of hope. By consistently putting one foot in front of the other, he encourages others to do the same. One twelve-year-old friend of Hero's recently shared, "Hero will always be my favorite horse because he proves that what seems impossible isn't.

And he helps me when I miss my brother who's in the National Guard. When I sit on Hero's back and know that he made it through his wilderness, I feel close to my brother and know he'll make it through his wilderness in Afghanistan too." Meanwhile, a farrier recognized Hero from a media report and identified the owner. The man who shot Hero twice in the head was located, arrested, tried, and convicted.

"The Smile"—My friend Misheal continues to beam the light and hope of Jesus. Miraculously, now forty years later, the blond girl who saved her life with just one smile a day has been located. After the release of this book, a copy will be anonymously sent to her with a card tucked into the chapter of "The Smile," informing her that *she* is the blue-eyed girl. A surprise reunion is currently being planned. I hope this makes readers ponder if it might be them! If not, it's never too late to begin smiling. Maybe someday someone will contact you to share the wonder of how

your gift provided unexpected hope.

"The Fall"—By our God's great mercy, Joan and I continue to be very dear friends. Although she has moved from Alaska to Vermont, and I live in Oregon, we spend as much time together as we can. We have many years of friendship and adventuring to make up for... and neither of us intends to miss a single one.

"The Scar"—Sweet little Angela came and visited the ranch one more time after our initial visit when she shared about her tremendous loss. She stayed long enough to let me know that I was right; she was making it through her grief, and she'd found a wonderful place to live. She also wanted to thank me for sharing with her the hope of Jesus. She now understands that because of Him, there will come a day when she too will see her scars as beauty marks.

"The Race"—After completing the U.S. Olympic Biathlon Team Trials, I never raced again. Although skating is still a big part of my life, and I ski every chance I get, this has now transformed into a time of exercise, reflection, and prayer. It seems that the voice I once heard echoing from an intrepid woman race official, I now hear ringing through the years as the voice of my beloved King:

   Go, girl! Go! Don't you ever quit!

DISCUSSION QUESTIONS

PART 1: THE PROBLEM

1. What matters most to you? What things tend to sidetrack you from becoming all that God is calling you to be?

2. You may never have found yourself clinging precariously to the side of a mountain, but perhaps you've encountered circumstances just as intense. What were the choices that led you there? How did God meet you in those situations?

3. In chapter 3, Kim wrote, "Authentic beauty is revealed in what we do for those in need around us. On that day I wanted to be beautiful like Amelia…because she was beautiful like Jesus." When was the last time you did something strictly for the benefit of someone else—knowing the person could not pay you back? Describe how you felt afterward.

4. What have you found to be the most effective ways of defending your heart against sin? What are some "arrows" you've encountered when you've let your guard down? As Kim pointed out, there is no arrow that the unfailing love of Jesus cannot remove. In a few words how would you describe His arrow-removing process in your life?

PART 2: THE KING

1. Kim says, "At some point we will all experience our best-laid plans being obliterated in a single moment. An accident, a disease, an addiction, an infidelity, a discovery, a choice—each can exact life-changing consequences." How has God shown His faithfulness to you in times like these?

2. Have you ever experienced total peace despite tumultuous or scary circumstances? If so, how would you advise a friend to find peace in the midst of troubled circumstances?

3. In chapter 11, Kim recalled God speaking to her: "The things you choose to entrust to Me, you will have *forever*. But the things that you choose to hold on to will all perish." What have you entrusted to God? What are you holding on to? Why? How are you protecting those things better than God could? When might you be willing to give those things to God as well?

4. Have you ever had a "wilderness" experience in which you didn't know how or when you'd make it through? What are your thoughts about where God is during those times? What was most effective in helping you put one foot in front of the other and not give up?

Part 3: The Warrior

1. Have you ever asked, "Who am I, and what do I really have to give?" Describe some things you've already given, such as a smile, a prayer, a word of encouragement, a small gift. Since you are unique and strategically placed in this world—no one else can be you— what are the gifts you have that can make a difference for those in your life who might be struggling?

2. In chapter 15, Kim compared unforgiveness to a prison. She also stated, "Forgiveness is a purposeful decision to let go of our years of rubble." Is there someone in your life you haven't fully forgiven? If you are holding on to years of rubble, what is it costing you? Are you willing to take action to be completely free?

3. In your own race through life, what weights slow you down? Who is cheering you on? Whom are you cheering for? What is your greatest motivation to do your best?

4. Kim wrote that a warrior is one who casts down her "princess crown" of entitlement and picks up her King's sword of encouragement to fiercely defend those who are losing their battle for hope. Consider your world, your community, your friends, your family. Of those near you, who is losing the battle for hope? If you were to pick up your sword of encouragement, what would that look like for the people around you?

ABOUT THE AUTHOR

KIM MEEDER is the cofounder and director of Crystal Peaks Youth Ranch (crystalpeaksyouthranch.org), an organization that rescues abused and dying horses and pairs them with children in need. Kim's first book, *Hope Rising,* propelled the ranch to win the national Jacqueline Kennedy Onassis Award and launched her extensive inspirational-speaking schedule at schools, churches, and governmental conferences across the United States. Together, Kim and her husband, Troy, have helped to establish nearly two hundred similar ranch ministries that serve children through horses. She and her husband have been married for thirty years and live in Central Oregon. The size of their family fluctuates each year with the number of horses and children they rescue.

HOPE IS FOR EVERYONE

Hope is like the stars—always there, yet shining brightest
in the blackest nights.

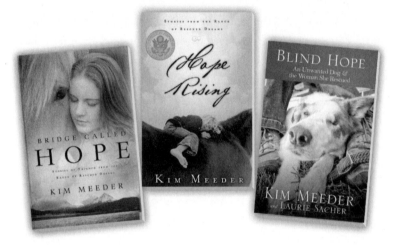

Experience more of Kim Meeder in these engaging
true-life stories of hope and selfless love.